BEHAVIORAL ACTIVATION FOR PTSD
A Workbook for Men

Behavioral Activation for PTSD

A WORKBOOK FOR MEN

Reduce Anxiety and Take Charge of Your Life

LISA BURGERT CAMPBELL, PHD

with Karie A. Kermath

ALTHEA
PRESS

For the veterans who have graciously shared their experiences with me, and for Mom, Dad, Grandma, Colin II, Colin III, and Nicholas. —LBC

For my parents, Anthony, Lisa, Kerri, and everyone who lifted me up when I lay shattered on the floor; for Chris, who held my hand; for Calvin, whose boundless love and resilience gave me hope. —KAK

Cover and Interior Designer: Katy Brown
Editor: Camille Hayes
Production Editor: Erum Khan

ISBN: Print 978-1-64152-075-1 | eBook 978-1-64152-076-8

CONTENTS

SECTION 6
HEALTH AND WELLNESS 127

SECTION 7
STAYING THE COURSE 152

FOREWORD

I AM PARTICULARLY HONORED to contribute the foreword to *Behavioral Activation for PTSD: A Workbook for Men*, not only because Dr. Lisa Campbell is a colleague of more than 15 years, but also because I have firsthand experience with her expertise in treating PTSD. As a combat veteran, I have struggled with many of the challenges and symptoms this workbook tackles and have been fortunate to have Dr. Campbell's guidance in helping me understand my problems and find ways to successfully confront them.

Stress from trauma has been around for a long time. In my years working for the US Department of Veterans Affairs, I have watched our understanding of PTSD evolve, so that we now know PTSD symptoms are normal reactions to an abnormal event: trauma. However, if those symptoms persist, they can cause people serious difficulties functioning in their day-to-day lives at home, at work or school, and in their relationships.

As a Gulf War veteran, US Army chaplain, and member of the PTSD clinical team in the Veterans Affairs San Diego Healthcare System, I understand the serious challenges men can face in the wake of trauma. This book is for anyone who is tired of letting PTSD disrupt their lives and wants to feel happier, more fulfilled, and more at peace. With work and practice, you can gradually reengage with the people and activities that give your life meaning and unlearn the crippling habits of avoidance we adopt after trauma in an effort to keep ourselves "safe." Not only do those avoidance strategies fail to protect us from the anxiety, panic, and depression PTSD can cause, they also cut us off from friends, family, and the simple joys of life. *Behavioral Activation for PTSD: A Workbook for Men* will help you chart a path out of the darkness and back toward the things you love most.

The authors of this workbook have written an easy-to-follow set of practical exercises that help you understand where you are in your recovery process, and how to move forward toward better health and healing. Because each section is structured around a major life domain—home life, work life, social and recreational life, and health and wellness—you'll find support no matter what challenges you're up against or where the path of recovery takes you in the future. In working through the exercises, you may come to realize that PTSD is impacting you in more ways than you first thought. But by practicing the skills in this book, you'll also discover that change is possible and relief is at hand.

If you apply the teachings in this book, they will help you chart your individual path to healing from the effects of your trauma. The exercises presented here will teach you to use your personal values to determine what recovery looks like for you—then use scientifically tested and proven-effective techniques to get you there. The authors write from experience and the wisdom gained over years of helping trauma survivors learn to apply effective coping strategies. They have created a workbook that will teach you the skills you need to survive and thrive. I believe that *Behavioral Activation for PTSD: A Workbook for Men* represents a breakthrough in treatment. It can and should become an indispensable guidebook for the millions of men dealing with the aftereffects of trauma, and an innovative tool for the professionals who work with them.

CHAPLAIN HENRY L. PETERSON, Lt. Colonel, United States Army, Retired

INTRODUCTION

IF YOU'RE HOLDING THIS BOOK, you have probably experienced something traumatic in your past that is causing you to struggle today. After dealing with a trauma, you may have noticed changes in your thoughts and emotional reactions. You might feel as if you're in a state of constant hypervigilance, staying on guard even in unthreatening situations. You might fixate on your traumatic memories and be unable to stop thinking about them, or your memory may have some blank spots that you can't fill no matter how hard you try.

This is how our brains learn to avoid future trauma and make sense of what has happened. Sometimes this process works, but sometimes we develop symptoms that are excessive, overwhelming, and debilitating. You may worry that the reactions you're having demonstrate weakness or that you're "going crazy." The fact is that your reactions might be symptoms of post-traumatic stress disorder (PTSD), and there are well-researched, proven methods available to help manage whatever trauma-related symptoms you may be struggling with. This workbook will guide you through one of those treatments: behavioral activation. Using this approach, you will get your life back on track by changing your behavior one step at a time.

As a clinical psychologist, I've spent the past 15 years working with veterans—most of them men—who have experienced the full range of traumatic events: combat, physical assault, rape, natural disaster, childhood trauma, and accidents. After working closely with so many men, I have learned that there are as many reactions to trauma as there are roads to recovery. Our brains are resilient, and with the proper tools, we can heal from PTSD.

My coauthor, Karie, also brings special insight to this project. After experiencing a family trauma, she developed PTSD. Like many of you, her symptoms increased over time until it was impossible for her to live a normal, satisfying life. She sought help and, after several months of intensive PTSD therapy, she's no longer haunted by intrusive thoughts, anxiety, and overwhelming anger. She understands the healing process from the inside out.

While this workbook will be helpful for anyone who has experienced trauma, we've chosen to focus on the unique experiences of men living with PTSD, because my years of working in Veterans Administration (VA) settings have taught me that men need more resources that speak to their unique perspective. Many historically male-dominated professions like military service, emergency response, and emergency medicine have a higher-than-average chance of being exposed to traumatic events. Although men are more likely than women to experience traumatic events in their lifetimes, they are less likely to recognize the symptoms and seek treatment for PTSD. This book aims to change that by providing an easy-to-use resource designed to help you understand your symptoms and plot a course toward recovery.

HOW TO USE THIS BOOK

MAYBE YOU'VE BEEN EXPERIENCING nightmares or panic attacks. Maybe you feel emotionally numb or excessively angry. Whatever your symptoms, with this workbook you'll learn how traumatic experiences change your ability to think, feel, and respond in many different types of situations. As you work through the exercises in this book, you'll discover that the best way to relieve your symptoms and reverse the damage caused by your traumatic experience is to meet your challenges head-on, whenever and wherever they arise.

The first section of this book provides general information about PTSD and describes its various symptoms. It includes checklists designed to help you identify areas where you're functioning well, along with areas you might want to address by learning new skills and coping strategies. The second section introduces you to the ins and outs of behavioral activation and provides a number of exercises to get you started.

The next four sections are structured around four main areas, or life domains, where your PTSD symptoms may be showing up: home life, work life, social and recreational life, and health and wellness. These sections are designed to help you figure out where you may be experiencing difficulties and provide strategies tailored to those particular areas of your life.

You can take the domain sections in any order, but it's recommended that you eventually complete all sections of the book to get the most improvement. It's possible that you've only noticed one or two symptoms, but the effects of trauma can impact you in sneaky ways that you might not recognize right away. As you work through this book and your awareness increases, you may discover that PTSD is showing up in places you hadn't noticed before.

By completing each section, you can ensure that you've done a thorough search for all possible symptoms needing attention. Because you may want to practice these exercises more than once, it's a good idea to make some copies of the exercises before you fill them out in the workbook.

The final section of the book is focused on helping you stay the course with useful exercises to keep you moving forward.

This workbook can also be used as a resource for someone who is trying to understand changes they've noticed in a loved one who has experienced trauma. While it's not intended to offer a clinical diagnosis and isn't a substitute for an assessment by an experienced professional, this book can be used as a guide to help initiate conversations with your loved one about what they're going through. From there, you may be better able to understand their experience and offer your support.

UNDERSTANDING PTSD

WHAT IS PTSD?

It's important to understand that PTSD is a set of normal, even predictable, responses to abnormal experiences. These responses—or symptoms—are the way our brain tries to make sense of what happened and help us avoid future situations that might cause more trauma. Maybe you're recovering from a one-time event like an assault, an accident, or the death of a loved one. Perhaps traumatic experiences are an inherent part of your occupation, as they are for first responders, military personnel, and some medical professionals. Or maybe you were a victim of domestic violence or child abuse, and trauma was a chronic part of your daily life. It's even possible that you have experienced multiple traumatic events in your life. Whatever your particular experience, your brain has found ways to adapt and worked out strategies to try to keep you safe from future harm.

Please note that just because someone has been exposed to trauma doesn't mean they'll go on to develop PTSD. Instead, PTSD occurs when a person has experienced trauma and then develops symptoms that significantly change the way they function in multiple life areas over time. In the aftermath of trauma, most early changes occur as a normal part of the healing process and resolve without treatment as the person processes the experience and moves forward. However, if the symptoms persist and continue to develop, PTSD may be identified as an ongoing problem that is causing challenges in day-to-day functioning. Unfortunately, when struggling with PTSD, many of the coping strategies people adopt to "feel better" in the short term actually increase the number or intensity of their symptoms over time.

It's not always clear why some people recover rapidly from trauma and others struggle for a longer time. But there are some well-established factors that influence the severity and persistence of trauma-related symptoms. These include your previous life experience, the nature of the trauma, and the types of coping strategies you use to manage your symptoms in the short term.

Men and PTSD

Men are 33 percent more likely than women to experience trauma, mostly because there are more men than women working in high-risk occupations. The most common causes of PTSD for men are physical assaults, severe accidents, combat exposure, and witnessing the severe injury or death of others. However, despite their increased risk of trauma, men are about 50 percent less likely to be diagnosed with PTSD. Some of this is probably due to the different *types* of trauma men and women typically experience, and whether the specific type of trauma is likely to lead them to seek professional help and therefore be diagnosed with PTSD. For example, in both men and women, sexual trauma is more likely to result in PTSD, but women are sexually assaulted at significantly higher levels than men. With that said, men with interpersonal traumas report fewer symptoms and still present for treatment less frequently than women. It's possible that this is accounted for by differences in male and female physiology and gender differences in how traumatic experience is processed or reported.

Of course, it's also possible that socialization and cultural expectation play a strong role in how men respond to trauma and how they understand and label their experience. Men are often told or expected to "suck it up" or "be a man." In professions where traumatic experience is the norm, there can be a lot of pressure to move forward and continue functioning without taking the time to process the impact of these difficult experiences. This ability to keep going in spite of a traumatic event can be critical to successfully performing jobs where immediate action is necessary, such as police, firefighting, or military jobs. Unfortunately, despite an increasing understanding of the monumental impact trauma has on the brain, many men refuse to acknowledge any changes they notice in their feelings or behaviors or seek assistance because they fear being labeled as incompetent.

Finally, since many men haven't been conditioned to talk about their emotions or their struggles, they may turn to unhealthy coping strategies to help numb their feelings and continue functioning day to day. These can include using alcohol or drugs, gambling, or engaging in risky sex to deflect the horror of their experience. While these strategies may be useful for coping with their professional life, they may cause significant problems in other areas. And it may only be as a man returns to a nonwork or civilian environment that he, and those around him, notice problems in daily functioning.

MAJOR SYMPTOMS OF PTSD

The major symptoms of PTSD include arousal (anxiety, anger, and panic attacks/physiological responses), depression, and intrusion (flashbacks, intrusive thoughts, and nightmares). In addition, extreme avoidance behavior, which includes escape and safety behaviors, is another major symptom—one that most likely impacts you on a daily basis. Because of this, in later sections, we're going to delve deep into how avoidance behaviors may be impacting each area of your life.

Even having one of the major symptoms of PTSD would be enough to make you wonder if you might be "going crazy." But when you put a few of them together, leading a normal life becomes a continuous struggle. The following are some brief descriptions and exercises to help you discover which of these symptoms are burdening you.

Arousal

Humans have evolved with a fight, flight, or freeze response to help us recognize and protect ourselves from danger. Physiological arousal in response to danger is normal and can save your life. However, traumatic experience can damage this system, leaving you with unneeded physiological responses that can be triggered by a "false alarm"—when you react to a safe situation as if it's dangerous or you have a really big response to a minor threat. It can also present chronically, like if you feel you've had too much caffeine when you haven't had any. Arousal symptoms can include feeling on edge, exaggerated startle responses, difficulty with concentration, anger and irritability, feelings of panic, and difficulty falling or staying asleep.

ANXIETY

Marshall was an eleventh-grade English teacher when there was a shooting at his school. Now, he can't relax, even at home. He's chronically anxious and concerned about safety. He's installed additional locks on all of his doors and security cameras that monitor everyone who comes and goes. Insomnia is now his nightly norm. After taking over an hour to fall asleep, he's awakened by any noise, including the brief click of the thermostat as the heater kicks on or his dog scratching in the middle of the night. And once he's awake, he can't go back to sleep until he's checked every door and window. Some nights he wakes up more than 20 times in eight hours.

Anxiety is the brain's way of responding to a perceived threat. One of the most common ways anxiety affects someone with PTSD is through hypervigilance, feeling the need to be on alert for danger at all times. However, there are many other indications that you might be suffering from anxiety. Maybe you startle easily when you hear a loud noise or someone suddenly appears beside you. You might feel nervous or restless, or have trouble sleeping because you wake in a panic with every sound. You may even have trouble concentrating or focusing on things that came easily to you in the past.

ANGER

Saul was always friendly and got along well with others before his trauma. Lately his wife complains that he's never in a good mood anymore. He's irritable and gets extremely upset over little things, like when she forgets to pick up something from the store or makes his toast too crispy. She avoids telling him about things that might bother him, like when they were overcharged by their cable company. Last weekend, they went to the mall, and Saul got into a confrontation in the parking lot when someone cut him off. He jumped out of the car and pounded on the hood of the other car. His wife was crying when he returned to the car and said that she was terrified by the whole incident. He's noticed that she's becoming more distant and increasingly willing to do activities without him, stating that it's easier and that she knows he's not interested anyway.

Anger is a normal, healthy emotion that everyone experiences. It tells us that our boundaries have been violated and energizes us to fight for our survival when we face a threat. However, after trauma, a minor threat can trigger you to react as if your survival is at stake. You may become easily provoked and respond at a level inappropriate for the situation. You may express your anger in outbursts or contain your anger but feel irritable. Some people suffering from PTSD report feeling a constant, burning anger that's not related to anything happening in the present moment.

Chronic anger can contribute to interpersonal difficulties and poor self-esteem. You may feel like you can't trust anyone or that others are "out to get you." You may try to control others in a variety of situations and then get angry with them if they don't follow your rules or suggestions. You may worry that you can't control your anger forever and will eventually explode, hurting those around you.

PANIC ATTACKS/PHYSIOLOGICAL RESPONSES

Theo wanted to attend his 20-year high school reunion, but he gets extremely uncomfortable in confined spaces and hasn't flown since having a work-related accident. Before the flight, he anticipated discomfort, but he was completely unprepared for just how awful it would be. He began perspiring as soon as he boarded the plane and felt his chest tighten as he fastened his seat belt. As the plane took off, he began breathing rapidly and the passengers seated next to him became visibly concerned. He had a similar experience once before and thought he was having a heart attack. During that episode, his friends called 911, but the ER staff told him his heart was healthy and that he'd experienced a panic attack.

While panic attacks are technically not a symptom of PTSD, they can co-occur. Even if you aren't having actual panic attacks, the physiological responses to trauma are similar enough that you might think that's what's happening. You may have trouble sleeping or feel nervous or restless for no reason. You might feel like you've had too many cups of coffee, even when you haven't had any. Maybe you have shortness of breath, chest pain, nausea, an accelerated heart rate, dizziness, or muscle tension. Some of these reactions can be very intense and come on suddenly, or you may experience them much of the time.

The acute anxiety of a panic attack can be terrifying. These episodes are the body's response to a perceived threat, and a traumatic experience can predispose you to respond this way when you encounter a trigger. Physiological responses associated with acute anxiety include excessive sweating, shaking/trembling, a feeling of impending doom, dizziness, chest pain, hyperventilation, and a rapid heart rate.

EXERCISE AROUSAL CHECKLIST

The following is a checklist of common arousal symptoms. Place a check mark in the box next to each symptom you've experienced. If you have two or more of these symptoms, arousal is probably causing you significant distress.

☐ Feeling very upset or panicked when something reminds you of the stressful experience

☐ Panic attacks/physiological responses to reminders of the trauma, including excessive sweating, rapid heart rate, shortness of breath, dizziness, nausea, and muscle tension

☐ Difficulty sleeping

☐ Irritability and/or anger

☐ Being on guard or hyperalert for danger; being preoccupied about safety issues

☐ Feeling jumpy or being easily startled

☐ Difficulty concentrating or maintaining focus

☐ Being restless, keyed up, on edge, nervous

Depression

Before George retired 11 months ago, he relied on his career to distract him from painful memories of his service in Vietnam. After so many years of working long hours, he and his wife made plans to travel, see friends, and spend time with their grandchildren. He looked forward to completing some woodworking projects and updating the landscaping around their house. However, instead of doing any of these things, George spends most of his time thinking about events that occurred 50 years ago. His wife has been patient, but she has started complaining that he just sits around the house and has given up on their retirement plans. He knows he has a lifetime of things to be thankful for, but he just can't find the energy or motivation to do anything and the things he used to enjoy don't interest him at all.

Many people know someone who suffers from depression, so you may already be familiar with this major PTSD symptom. It's generally characterized by persistent feelings of sadness, which may also include a loss of interest in usual activities, lack of motivation, fatigue, feelings of hopelessness or worthlessness, changes in appetite, loss of interest in sex, inappropriate guilt, emotional numbing, social isolation, self-harming behaviors or urges, and thoughts of death or suicide.

EXERCISE   DEPRESSION CHECKLIST

The following is a checklist of common depression symptoms. Place a check mark in the box next to each symptom you've experienced. If you have two or more of these symptoms, depression is probably causing you significant distress.

☐ Loss of enjoyment in regular activities

☐ Feeling distant from others or socially isolating yourself

☐ Feeling numb or unable to feel a full range of feelings

☐ Lack of motivation

☐ Fatigue

☐ Feeling hopeless or worthless

☐ Changes in appetite

☐ Loss of interest in sex

☐ Inappropriate feelings of guilt or shame

☐ Difficulty trusting others

☐ Thoughts of suicide or self-harm*

IMPORTANT: If you have thoughts of suicide or self-harm, turn now to page 160 and fill out the Safety Plan. We care about you and want you to be safe.

Intrusion

As your brain attempts to make sense of a traumatic experience, it repeatedly processes the things that happened to you. Traumatic experiences are a problem for our brain because these events fall outside our previous experience. In the struggle to "understand," our brain keeps trying to organize the memories. Most often, people suffering from PTSD experience this processing as intrusive thoughts and nightmares. Very rarely, someone may experience a flashback.

INTRUSIVE THOUGHTS AND FLASHBACKS

Every year on the Fourth of July, Javier's friends and family get together for a barbecue and to watch the fireworks from his parents' backyard. The first year after he returned from the Middle East, he was surprised when the fireworks started and they brought up such vivid memories of his combat experience that he became disoriented. He became so visibly upset that his mom took him inside to the basement and sat with her arms wrapped around him until the fireworks ended. In the years since, even though he knows what to expect, he comes for the barbecue, assures his mom he's fine, and then excuses himself before the fireworks start. He sits in the basement petting his parents' dog until the show is over.

Intrusive thoughts are involuntary, repeated, very distressing, unwanted thoughts and memories that are related to your trauma and difficult to predict. Attempts to force them from your mind are often ineffective and may actually increase their frequency and intensity. They may impact you when you're sitting quietly by yourself or in the middle of an important conversation or meeting.

You may even think about the things you wish you'd done differently during your traumatic event. Or you may feel guilty if you don't think about other people who were part of your traumatic experience. Internal reminders of trauma, such as anniversary dates, or external event reminders, such as people, places, or things, might increase your intrusive thoughts and nightmares (discussed next).

Less commonly, you may experience a flashback, which is an episode in which you feel as if you're physically reliving the traumatic experience. If you've ever experienced a full flashback, it was bound to be frightening for you and anyone around you. Fortunately, these episodes are rare, but because you act as if you are actually reliving the traumatic experience, they are extremely disturbing.

NIGHTMARES

Ang is a police officer and has responded to many violent crime scenes. He likes his job but can't stop thinking about memories that he wishes he could forget. His symptoms are worse at night, and he frequently wakes up, shaking and in a cold sweat, because of bad dreams. After a hard shift, it takes him hours to fall asleep each night, and he awakens from terrifying nightmares.

Even if you're used to an active dream life, the vividness of PTSD nightmares might surprise you. Sometimes they're a direct replay of the traumatic event. Other times they may be indirectly related to the trauma. They may be accompanied by increased body movement, such as kicking, hitting, or writhing. You may call out or yell in your sleep. You may decide to sleep alone because you're afraid of disturbing or hurting a bed partner. It's common for trauma survivors to have several nightmares per week, for months or even years after the event.

EXERCISE   INTRUSION CHECKLIST

The following is a checklist of common intrusion symptoms. Place a check mark in the box next to each symptom you've experienced. If you have two or more of these symptoms, intrusion is probably causing you significant distress.

- ☐ Nightmares
- ☐ Flashbacks or feeling like you're reexperiencing the event
- ☐ Emotional or physical upset with external reminders of the event (e.g., sights, sounds, smells)

- ☐ Distress with internal reminders of the event (e.g., anniversary dates, memories)
- ☐ Unwanted, uncontrollable thoughts or memories

Avoidance

Lucas was assaulted one night while walking home from work. Before the assault, he'd always been confident and felt capable of protecting himself. Now he questions his safety constantly. He used to enjoy going out with friends. Now he stays away from crowded places or feels that he needs to drink a few beers first to feel comfortable. He's called in sick to work several times, particularly when scheduled to work late or if he doesn't have a ride home.

Avoiding danger is a basic human survival instinct. After trauma, your perception of danger can shift and generate a strong urge to avoid things that you previously enjoyed or believed to be safe. This could be a situation that triggers your symptoms and makes you feel an overwhelming need to escape, even though you know there's no actual threat. You may also attempt to avoid or escape your emotions or memories with distracting habitual behaviors, such as using alcohol or drugs, or by implementing new or extreme safety measures. Avoidance may start with people, places, or things (sights, smells, sounds, objects, etc.) associated with the traumatic experience, but it can expand to include many of the activities associated with daily life.

EXERCISE AVOIDANCE CHECKLIST

The following is a checklist of common avoidance symptoms. Place a check mark in the box next to each symptom you've experienced. If you have two or more of these symptoms, avoidance behavior is probably causing you significant distress.

☐ Efforts to avoid thinking or talking about the trauma

☐ Efforts to avoid people, places, things (e.g., sights, smells, sounds that remind you of the trauma)

☐ Staying busy to avoid thinking

☐ Using habitual behaviors to distract (e.g., drugs, alcohol, video gaming)

☐ Adopting new or extreme safety habits (e.g., security cameras, alarms, additional locks, refusal to leave home without a weapon, sleeping with a gun or knife under your pillow)

☐ Avoiding crowded places

☐ Avoiding media coverage or entertainment related to the trauma (e.g., books, movies, television, internet)

☐ Needing to be in control at all times (e.g., refusal to be a passenger in a car, unwillingness to be a subordinate, inability to live spur of the moment)

☐ Restricting/monitoring activities of loved ones (e.g., not allowing children to go on sleepovers or play at others' homes, constantly checking up on safety and whereabouts of loved ones)

WHAT CAUSES PTSD?

Trauma is an unexpected, threatening event that either happens to you or that you witness happening to someone else. This event may involve actual or threatened death, but it doesn't have to. Some examples of traumatic events include:

- Rape or sexual assault (including attempted assault)
- Physical assault/violence
- Combat
- Natural disaster
- Accidents (e.g., automotive, aircraft, work-related)
- Unexpected death of a loved one
- Serious accidental injury
- Near-death experience
- Domestic violence or abuse
- Childhood neglect or abuse
- Work as a first responder or emergency medical personnel
- Community violence/gang violence
- Repeated exposure to upsetting details of someone else's trauma

Maybe you've experienced more than one trauma during your life. The more traumatic experiences a person has, even if the types of trauma are very different, the more challenging recovery can be. If your trauma occurred during childhood, you may have a harder time recognizing that things you do now are reactions to that early trauma.

Trauma's Lingering Effects

Individuals who have experienced trauma can have a variety of lingering effects. Trauma can fundamentally shift the way we think, the way we feel, and what we do. Some of the lasting impacts may include:

- Work problems, such as difficulty getting and maintaining jobs, problems with coworkers and supervisors, and overworking
- Family relationship issues, such as challenges with family members, divorce, and family estrangement
- Conflicts with family members, friends, coworkers, roommates, and neighbors; problems with anger
- Addictive/habit-forming behaviors, such as drinking alcohol, doing drugs, gambling, engaging in risky sex, viewing pornography, overspending, and overeating
- Thrill-seeking/reckless behaviors and activities, such as driving too fast, extreme sports, fighting, impulsivity, unprotected sex, and binge drinking
- Suicidal thoughts or self-injurious behaviors

- Problems with authority
- Difficulty establishing trust in relationships
- Excessive or inappropriate guilt and/or shame
- Questioning spirituality
- Difficulty forgiving self or others
- Isolating or avoiding activity; disengaging from friends and family
- Legal problems, such as DUI or arrest for fighting
- Changes in how others respond to you

Your Brain on Trauma

Last year, Jerome was mugged. Recently he's noticed that he startles when someone approaches him from behind. It takes a long time for his heart rate and breathing to return to normal. Last week, while he was focused on completing a project in his front yard, someone bumped into him from behind. He almost hit the person before realizing it was his young daughter who accidentally ran into him while playing. He doesn't understand why he's become so sensitive to situations that he knew were safe in the past. He knows the danger isn't real, but he can't control his response.

Think of your brain as the early warning system that protects you from threatening situations. When triggered, it initiates a fear response designed to make you fight, flee, or freeze. Trauma can damage your brain so significantly that its early warning system no longer functions properly.

Like Jerome, many trauma survivors struggle to distinguish a safe situation from a dangerous one. This is because the part of the brain that interprets your environment is no longer able to assess a realistic level of current danger. On top of that, one of the main regions of the brain impacted by trauma is the part that regulates your emotional response. This can result in emotional reactions that are too strong or, on occasion, not strong enough.

And finally, when your brain activates the fear response, it releases hormones that trigger physiological reactions associated with stress, such as increased respiration, heart rate, and blood pressure. After trauma, these responses can become exaggerated and take longer to dissipate once a threat has been resolved.

Trauma survivors are also at an increased risk of developing other mental health disorders, such as depression and anxiety. But there is hope. Just as traumatic experiences can alter the structure of the brain, effective intervention can reverse those changes and alleviate symptoms.

DO YOU HAVE PTSD?

Not all trauma results in PTSD. All of the symptoms we've discussed are normal responses to a shocking or devastating event. After a trauma, people frequently experience these symptoms for a period of time as they recover. However, if your symptoms don't diminish after about a month's time, or if they get worse, they may need attention before you can start feeling better. It's also possible to experience these symptoms in response to other stressors that are not traumatic (painful relationship breakup, losing a job, caring for a family member during a long illness, etc.). In these cases, the symptoms aren't due to PTSD, but you may still benefit from self-help or professional help. If you've suffered a trauma and are having symptoms that increase or don't resolve over time, you may have PTSD.

EXERCISE   WHAT HAVE YOU NOTICED?

In the space provided, list the changes you or your loved ones have noticed about your behavior.

PUTTING IT ALL TOGETHER

Now it's time to take what you've learned, look at your responses to all of the exercises, and figure out which life domains are impacted by each symptom of PTSD you are experiencing. Place a check mark in the box under the life domain(s) you feel are impacted by that particular symptom. Blank lines are provided for you to fill in any symptoms you are having that aren't listed.

AROUSAL SYMPTOMS	HOME LIFE	WORK LIFE	SOCIAL AND RECREATIONAL LIFE	HEALTH AND WELLNESS
Feeling very upset or panicked when something reminds you of the stressful experience				
Panic attacks/physiological responses to reminders of the trauma, including excessive sweating, rapid heart rate, shortness of breath, dizziness, nausea, muscle tension				
Difficulty sleeping				
Irritability and/or anger				
Being on guard or hyperalert for danger, being preoccupied about safety issues				
Feeling jumpy or being easily startled				
Difficulty concentrating or maintaining focus				
Being restless, keyed up, on edge, nervous				
ADDITIONAL SYMPTOMS YOU'VE NOTICED:				

(CONTINUED)

DEPRESSION SYMPTOMS	HOME LIFE	WORK LIFE	SOCIAL AND RECREATIONAL LIFE	HEALTH AND WELLNESS
Loss of enjoyment in regular activities				
Feeling distant from others or socially isolating yourself				
Feeling numb or unable to feel a full range of emotions				
Lack of motivation				
Fatigue				
Feeling hopeless or worthless				
Changes in appetite				
Loss of interest in sex				
Inappropriate feelings of guilt or shame				
Difficulty trusting others				
Thoughts of suicide or self-harm				
ADDITIONAL SYMPTOMS YOU'VE NOTICED:				

INTRUSION SYMPTOMS	HOME LIFE	WORK LIFE	SOCIAL AND RECREATIONAL LIFE	HEALTH AND WELLNESS
Nightmares				
Flashbacks or feeling like you're reexperiencing the event				
Emotional or physical upset with external reminders of the event (e.g., sights, sounds, smells)				
Distress with internal reminders of the event (e.g., anniversary dates, memories)				
Unwanted, uncontrollable thoughts or memories				
ADDITIONAL SYMPTOMS YOU'VE NOTICED:				

(CONTINUED)

AVOIDANCE SYMPTOMS	HOME LIFE	WORK LIFE	SOCIAL AND RECREATIONAL LIFE	HEALTH AND WELLNESS
Efforts to avoid thinking or talking about the trauma				
Efforts to avoid people, place, things (e.g., sights, smells, sounds, objects) that remind you of the trauma				
Staying busy to avoid thinking				
Using habitual behaviors to distract (e.g., drugs, alcohol, video gaming)				
Adopting new or extreme safety habits (e.g., security cameras, alarms, additional locks, refusal to leave home without a weapon, sleeping with a gun or knife under your pillow)				
Avoiding crowded places				
Avoiding media coverage or entertainment related to the trauma (e.g., books, movies, television, internet)				
Needing to be in control at all times (e.g., refusal to be a passenger in a car, unwillingness to be a subordinate, inability to live spur of the moment)				
Restricting/monitoring activities of loved ones (e.g., not allowing children to go on sleepovers or play at others' homes, constantly checking up on the safety and whereabouts of loved ones)				
ADDITIONAL SYMPTOMS YOU'VE NOTICED:				

Are there particular areas where you seem to be experiencing more symptoms? Use the information in this worksheet to decide which life domains you need to tackle first, after you've completed section 2: Getting Active. You can skip right to the life domain that needs the most attention and start there—just be sure you complete all the sections eventually.

TAKEAWAYS

- There are well-researched, proven methods available for the treatment of PTSD.
- The major symptoms of PTSD include arousal (anxiety, anger, and panic attacks/physiological responses), depression, intrusion (flashbacks, intrusive thoughts, and nightmares), and avoidance.
- PTSD is caused by an unexpected, threatening event that happens to you or you witness happening to someone else.
- Men are more likely than women to experience trauma, but less likely to recognize trauma-related symptoms or seek treatment.
- Trauma survivors can experience lingering effects in various life domains, including home life, work life, social and recreational life, and health and wellness.

GETTING ACTIVE

WHAT IS BEHAVIORAL ACTIVATION?

Think about one of your daily habits. Whether you feel like you can't start your morning without a brisk run or drinking a cup of coffee and reviewing last night's sport scores, you developed your habit over time because it gave you some kind of satisfaction or positive benefit. Of course, habits can be good, but they can also be harmful. No one starts out downing a six-pack of beer every night. They start with an occasional drink after a long day of work and gradually develop a nightly habit that becomes more and more ingrained over time.

After a trauma, it's normal to notice changes in your habits and interests. Maybe you've lost the enthusiasm for doing things you used to enjoy or developed a new behavior that makes it easier for you to forget the trauma for a little while. It may be that you don't feel like doing anything at all. Things like avoiding some of your normal activities may seem to work in the short term and bring you a little relief.

But as you develop avoidance behaviors, your natural *reinforcement* process—that is, the positive outcomes you experience that make you want to do something again—is interrupted because you miss out on all of the good things you were doing before. This lack of natural reinforcement can lead to depression or demotivation, as you come to feel that life has nothing good or rewarding to offer. All this can make it downright challenging to stay active and involved in your life.

On the other hand, when we do something that makes us feel good—like attending one of those social events PTSD makes us want to avoid—our mood improves and we might even feel a sense of accomplishment. As we repeat the same activity and reexperience those good feelings, our brain links them together, and we begin to develop a habit. This natural reinforcement is something that happens without our even realizing it.

Behavioral activation is a process that takes advantage of our brain's natural tendencies to respond to pleasurable experiences and to form associations. Think of it as therapy for the behaviors you want to change. It capitalizes on the natural reinforcement you get from doing things that make you feel good, like physical activity, socializing, or participating in your hobbies.

Over time, behavioral activation encourages repeated participation in activities that create positive feelings—these are your "target behaviors" and will be very important as you create your plan for change. In addition, this strategy is especially useful at addressing avoidance behaviors (e.g., drinking, extreme safety checks, isolation) that have been reinforced until they've become problematic habits that are difficult to shake. Right now, by learning to wield the tool of behavioral activation, you can start to improve your symptoms, broaden your range of activities, and enjoy life again.

One of the biggest challenges of resuming an active life is stepping out of your comfort zone. The extreme and/or long-term stress you experience after a trauma can damage your fight, flight, or freeze response and cause frequent false alarms. If your brain can no longer accurately assess levels of danger, you tend to respond to relatively safe situations as if they're threatening. Things that you used to enjoy or places you used to visit may no longer feel safe. Eventually, you start avoiding any situation that triggers these endless and exhausting false alarms. As the avoidance response is reinforced by the short-term relief you feel, it becomes more and more difficult to do anything.

The First Step

Since Nathaniel left the navy 13 months ago, his life hasn't gone the way he planned. When anticipating his discharge, he looked forward to starting a new job and getting married to his high school sweetheart. However, he quickly became frustrated with coworkers and supervisors who always seemed to be cutting corners and ignoring safety regulations. It was too stressful so he quit to go back to college.

But his classes didn't prove to be much better. He struggled to concentrate during class and had trouble finding common ground with the other students. He dropped two of his courses after missing too many classes and falling behind. In addition, his relationship didn't work out, and he's not ready to start dating. His friends try to be supportive, but he wonders if they have anything in common anymore. He rarely agrees to see them and has even stopped going to his weekly poker game. He used to enjoy basketball and eating out with friends, but it seems like too much work to put a game together or schedule a dinner out with others. Most days, Nathaniel stays home alone. His laundry and unopened bills are piling up, and he hasn't gone grocery shopping in weeks.

The first step of behavioral activation is to look at your daily choices and figure out how they impact your quality of life. Then, you can make smart decisions about what you want your life to look like in the future and what you need to do to get there. We'll guide you through this process in later workbook exercises.

This doesn't mean that you'll attempt to change your behavior all at once. Imagine if you were afraid of heights and wanted to be comfortable climbing a ladder. Behavioral activation doesn't ask you to conquer your fear by trekking Mount Everest. Not only would that be ridiculous, it would be extremely unpleasant. Instead, it asks you to take small steps toward your goal, such as climbing on the second or third rung of a ladder to get used to the feeling. Over a period of time, you'd practice going higher and higher until you were comfortable going all the way to the top. Of course, if your secret desire were to make it to the top of Mount Everest, behavioral activation could get you there. But you would still need to take one small step at a time to prepare for the summit.

With that said, you need to understand that even small steps might make you uncomfortable as you challenge yourself to change your habits. But the discomfort should be moderate, and it won't last forever. Even if there are moments you feel extremely uncomfortable, don't give up. You can always attempt a different challenge the next time you try. Trust us, this process works. And it works best when you push yourself to tackle one moderately difficult activity at a time and stick with it until it's no longer something you want to avoid or escape.

What Is It Used For?

Behavioral activation is a set of techniques originally used to treat depression. More recently, therapists have also started using it to treat PTSD. Like most effective treatments for mental health conditions, it's based on the idea that thoughts, behaviors, and emotions are all linked and that when you make a positive change in one of those areas, the others will also improve. Like the name suggests, behavioral activation focuses on changing your *behavior* by *activating* new behaviors, which results in changing the way you think and feel.

There are other cognitive and behavioral approaches to treating PTSD that focus on tackling the traumatic experiences directly. We will discuss these in greater detail later (see "Other PTSD Treatments" on page 22). However, despite their effectiveness, they only work if people complete the treatment programs. Their dropout rates are high, with only about 10 percent of veterans diagnosed with PTSD successfully completing one of the recommended treatments. The other 90 percent feel either unable to initiate treatment or to continue with the full course. And non-veterans suffering from PTSD have even fewer available options for treatment than their veteran counterparts. Cost of treatment, a lack of trained professionals in many communities, and the fact that many trauma survivors, understandably, don't feel prepared to repeatedly process their experience for weeks or even months at a time all make it very difficult to find or complete trauma-focused treatment. Clearly, there's a need to improve the options available for addressing symptoms of trauma.

That's where behavioral activation comes in. If you're apprehensive about trauma-focused treatment or don't want to directly confront your past experiences, behavioral activation is the right approach for you. As you take one step at a time toward reaching your goals, you'll start to feel better, and by the time you finish this workbook, you should be on the path toward living a healthier, more productive life. And once you've worked through our program, if you feel that more treatment is needed, you'll be better prepared to tackle a trauma-focused treatment head-on.

Does It Work?

From the very beginning of our existence, humans have experienced trauma. Yet, just 40 years ago, we still didn't understand why PTSD occurs or have a reliable way to treat its painful, disruptive symptoms. Since then, as our scientific knowledge has increased, so has our ability to treat this disorder. This has allowed many trauma survivors to return to active and satisfying lives. However, we must do more. Studies done on non-veteran populations are extremely rare, even for high-risk groups like first responders.

The good news is that recent studies indicate that behavioral activation works both with PTSD and the depressive symptoms that frequently occur in the aftermath of trauma. In a VA test of behavioral activation, more than half of participants showed a reduction in PTSD symptoms, and some also showed reductions in depressed mood. Overall, those who participated expressed a high level of satisfaction with their treatment experience. In addition, a case study in *Behavioural and Cognitive Psychotherapy* found that behavioral activation was successful in treating PTSD and depression in an individual who was a first responder as well as a military veteran and that these gains were maintained after treatment was completed.

Other PTSD Treatments

At some point, everyone who considers psycho-therapy wonders whether professional help is the right step for them. Many people go to extreme lengths to avoid thinking or talking about their traumatic experience, which can make them apprehensive about starting treatment. Maybe they feel they should be able to cope on their own or that needing help makes them weak. Maybe they believe that others have experienced more serious traumas and are more deserving of help.

Once the decision to seek help is made, the next step is deciding on a therapist and treatment approach. Competent professionals carry a variety of different credentials. including working as doctoral-level psychologists, nurse specialists, social workers, and masters-level counselors. Regardless of the type of professional or method chosen, finding a provider who specializes in treating trauma can be the key to success.

Over the last few decades, enormous progress in developing scientifically based interventions for PTSD has been made. These innovations can reduce the severity or frequency of trauma-related symptoms. In addition, once treatment has been completed, many people no longer meet criteria for PTSD. The National Center for PTSD has identified three of the best treatment practices, which all involve processing the traumatic memory and its meaning. These treatments are time-limited, generally consisting of 8 to 16 sessions.

Prolonged Exposure (PE) involves processing memories of the traumatic event during sessions with a therapist while confronting feared situations through personalized homework assignments.

Cognitive-Processing Therapy (CPT) consists of a careful examination of thoughts and feelings about the trauma. During treatment, errors in thinking are identified and corrected through discussion and a series of short written assignments.

Eye Movement Desensitization and Reprocessing (EMDR) allows the individual to reprocess traumatic memories while undergoing brain stimulation with eye-movement exercises.

Some approaches focus on helping you change the way you think about yourself, others, and the world. They can help you recognize areas where you may be overestimating risk or have thoughts that are overly influenced by your traumatic experience. After you identify the problematic thoughts, you will be encouraged to challenge them, and, as you shift your thinking, you may start feeling better and making healthier choices. Others involve directly confronting the traumatic memories and real-life situations that trigger distressing emotional reactions so you can learn that, while painful, those situations and memories aren't actually dangerous in the present.

PE, CPT, and EMDR are all extremely effective at reducing the symptoms of PTSD. However, they require you to extensively process your upsetting thoughts or feelings to reap their rewards. The benefit of a behavioral activation approach is that you don't have to think or feel any differently to get started. Instead, you focus on changing the problem behaviors, and ultimately find that your feelings and ideas about your trauma change too. By using this approach, things that were uncomfortable at first begin to get a little easier every time you practice.

Don't give up if you've tried treatment before without success. You may need to try a different type of therapy and/or find a new provider better suited to your personal needs.

How Will It Help You?

Behavioral activation helps alleviate trauma-related symptoms by getting you back to doing things that will naturally help you start feeling better. As you get moving with this program, you'll also challenge yourself to engage with people and things you value, exposing yourself to the activities you've been avoiding. Together, behavioral activation and exposure to things you've been avoiding are effective in the successful treatment of PTSD and depression.

Let's put this into perspective with an example of how you might have progressed from trauma to avoidance and/or depression. Perhaps after your traumatic experience, you went out to dinner or took your kids to the park, and you experienced an overwhelming level of anxiety. To escape or avoid those feelings, you changed or even cancelled upcoming plans. At that moment, you experienced immediate relief from your discomfort—namely, the discomfort/dread you felt in anticipation of being in a potentially anxiety-provoking situation.

But the cost of that relief resulted in the loss of pleasure you would have felt from, for example, meeting up with a friend or spending time with your kids. In addition, your avoidance also resulted in a loss of confidence in your ability to do those things in the future. This means that your anxiety increases every time you unsuccessfully approach that activity, meaning you will feel less confident in your ability to do it in the future. These feelings can ultimately lead to depression.

If you stop doing the things that bring you pleasure or a sense of accomplishment, you miss out on the natural reinforcement these activities provide. But if you resume an activity that you enjoy, your symptoms will likely begin to improve regardless of what you were thinking or how you were feeling when you did the activity. Positive reinforcers—the "rewards" that naturally occur in our lives—make you feel good when you encounter them, even if you started out feeling anxious or depressed. Behavioral activation offers the opportunity to address symptoms of depression, anxiety, and avoidance that are commonly experienced in the aftermath of trauma.

In the space provided, write about how PTSD is interfering with your life. You can make a list or write a short paragraph.

_____

_____

_____

_____

Next, in the space provided, write about what you want your life to look like after you've completed this workbook. Again, you can make a list or write a short paragraph.

_____

_____

_____

_____

This exercise helps you start bringing awareness to what's not working and gives you a goal to aspire to.

WHAT DO YOU WANT TO CHANGE?

If you're reading this book, it's probably because something in your life—your job, your family relationships, your social life—isn't going the way you want it to, and you'd like to change that. But what, exactly, is going wrong? Which aspects of your PTSD-related challenges are most important to address? You are the only one who can answer those questions, and the best way to find those answers is to take a look at your personal *values*.

Each of us has a unique set of values that helps us lead a meaningful life. Values are highly individual. For some people, a central life value might be physical fitness, while for others it could be participation in a faith community. Whatever your values are, they should reflect the things in life that are most important to you.

Values don't usually change much over time. However, even though they tend to be rather stable, our goals can shift substantially as we develop and experience new things, both good and bad. Think of your values as the path you choose to take rather than as your specific destination. For example, maybe for you, learning is an important value. Your goal might be to obtain a college degree or to complete an apprenticeship, or maybe you want to learn a new language or how to repair basic things around the house. Your *value* is learning, while your *goals* are the specific destinations you choose to visit on your learning path.

Deciding which direction to go, as determined by your values, is the first step in getting active. This can be difficult, especially if you feel like you've drifted away from your sense of purpose. Sometimes people feel like they've veered so far off course that it's pointless to return to the plans they had prior to their traumatic experience. If this sounds like you, don't worry—it's absolutely normal. You may naturally discover that what used to be important is no longer relevant at this stage of your life. That's why it's important to take a close look at your values as a first step toward getting you where you want to go. Once you identify your core values, you can begin selecting specific goals that make sense for you now. Then, as you complete one goal, you can start planning the next.

Sometimes it can be difficult to identify your personal values and goals because of the messages you receive from others about what they think you should value or achieve. Not only do well-meaning friends and family tell you what you should value and which goals you should set, but so does society. Telling the difference between what is important to you and what you think others expect you to do can be particularly tricky.

Completing a values assessment, which you'll do in the next exercise, gives you the opportunity to think about your life and plans in a way that might be new to you. Basically, it allows you to stop and check where you are in relation to your compass points, whatever they may be. Once you determine your current location and compare it with your target, you can adjust your trajectory and move in the valued direction.

Keep in mind that it's impossible to always move in a straight line toward your objectives. Things get in the way or sometimes we learn something new that forces us to reassess our plan. That's okay and should be expected. The important thing to remember is that you're undertaking this difficult challenge so that you can do more of the things you value in life. Keep checking in with your values and assessing your progress, making course corrections as needed if you find yourself getting a bit off track.

The series of exercises on the following pages are designed to help you figure out where to start and what you should focus on as you begin changing your behaviors. Once you've learned the skills in these exercises, you can apply them to any behaviors you want to change as you move on to the four life domain sections of this book.

EXERCISE   YOUR VALUES

Rate the values listed below by writing a number from 0 (not important at all) to 10 (extremely important) in the circle next to each value. It's okay to use the same numbers more than once. You can add additional values in the blank lines under the last circles. Here's an example:

10	7	6
Intimate Relationships	Friendships/Social Life	Education/Learning
10	9	4
Parenting	Financial Health	Community Service

( )	( )	( )
Physical Health	Spirituality	Education/Learning
( )	( )	( )
Recreation/Hobbies	Intimate Relationships	Community Service
( )	( )	( )
Work Life	Parenting	Emotional Health
( )	( )	( )
Home Life	Friendships/Social Life	....
( )	( )	( )
Family Life	Financial Health	....

What is most important to you? Write down your top three values in the space provided:

1. ....

2. ....

3. ....

As you move on to the next four sections, use the numbers you've assigned to each value to help decide which behaviors you should tackle first in each of the life domains. For example, if you highly value physical health, make a point to select goals that reflect that value.

LET'S GET TO WORK

Now that you've identified your core values, it's time to figure out what you're currently doing and what you want to change. This information will help you begin selecting your target behaviors and the goals, or steps, that will get you there. You'll then participate in tasks designed to help you reach your goals and learn how to schedule daily activities that align with your values and keep you accountable to yourself.

Of course, there will be challenges along the way. One potential roadblock might be finding the motivation or energy to keep going. And you will most certainly experience things that make you want to avoid or escape some situations. But as you move forward, you'll begin to develop problem-solving techniques and healthy coping strategies to manage any discomfort and stay motivated.

EXERCISE   WHAT ARE YOU DOING NOW?

Let's start with a disclaimer. This exercise may seem tedious, but it's essential to get a real and complete sense of how you're spending your time and what you're feeling when doing each activity. That way, you'll know what needs to change and what you're already doing well. You'll also have an activity log that will help you figure out where to insert new target activities as you begin working on attaining your goals.

It's up to you how often you fill in the information. You can keep a copy with you to update throughout the day, or you can fill it in all at once right before bed—whatever works best for you. If you lose track of a few hours, don't worry; just do your best to think back on what you were doing so you can fill in the missing time slots.

Observing how you're spending your time will let you recognize your unhealthy coping strategies as well as activities that bring a healthy sense of accomplishment. This exercise will help you move forward as you plan your personalized program.

Remember, this entire workbook is *your* tool—you can adapt it to your own needs. If you want to start tracking your activities today and wait to continue reading until after the entire seven days have passed, that's okay. However, it's also okay to start tracking today *and* continue reading. Our goal is to give you the tools you need to activate your behavior and reactivate your life. You should do what feels right, aiming for a moderate level of discomfort to increase your chance of success.

As you look at how you spend your time over the course of several days, you'll be able to assess how your current behaviors serve your values and current goals. You may discover areas where your activity has drifted far from your current goals. But you may also find areas of progress you hadn't previously identified, as well as healthy behaviors that you should engage in more regularly. Rate each pair of emotions on a scale of 0 to 10 (0 = a complete lack of the emotion, 10 = a high level of the emotion). Feel free to fill in the rating for other emotions you might experience that aren't included.

DAY ONE

DAY OF THE WEEK: DATE:

HOUR	ACTIVITY	DEPRESSION/ SADNESS	ANXIETY/ IRRITABILITY	PLEASURE/ SATISFACTION	OTHER
6 a.m.					
7 a.m.					
8 a.m.					
9 a.m.					
10 a.m.					
11 a.m.					
12 p.m.					
1 p.m.					
2 p.m.					
3 p.m.					
4 p.m.					
5 p.m.					
6 p.m.					
7 p.m.					
8 p.m.					
9 p.m.					
10 p.m.					
11 p.m.					
12 a.m.					
1 a.m.					
2 a.m.					
3 a.m.					
4 a.m.					
5 a.m.					

DAY TWO

DAY OF THE WEEK: DATE:

HOUR	ACTIVITY	DEPRESSION/ SADNESS	ANXIETY/ IRRITABILITY	PLEASURE/ SATISFACTION	OTHER
6 a.m.					
7 a.m.					
8 a.m.					
9 a.m.					
10 a.m.					
11 a.m.					
12 p.m.					
1 p.m.					
2 p.m.					
3 p.m.					
4 p.m.					
5 p.m.					
6 p.m.					
7 p.m.					
8 p.m.					
9 p.m.					
10 p.m.					
11 p.m.					
12 a.m.					
1 a.m.					
2 a.m.					
3 a.m.					
4 a.m.					
5 a.m.					

DAY THREE

DAY OF THE WEEK: DATE:

HOUR	ACTIVITY	DEPRESSION/ SADNESS	ANXIETY/ IRRITABILITY	PLEASURE/ SATISFACTION	OTHER
6 a.m.					
7 a.m.					
8 a.m.					
9 a.m.					
10 a.m.					
11 a.m.					
12 p.m.					
1 p.m.					
2 p.m.					
3 p.m.					
4 p.m.					
5 p.m.					
6 p.m.					
7 p.m.					
8 p.m.					
9 p.m.					
10 p.m.					
11 p.m.					
12 a.m.					
1 a.m.					
2 a.m.					
3 a.m.					
4 a.m.					
5 a.m.					

DAY FOUR

DAY OF THE WEEK: DATE:

HOUR	ACTIVITY	DEPRESSION/ SADNESS	ANXIETY/ IRRITABILITY	PLEASURE/ SATISFACTION	OTHER
6 a.m.					
7 a.m.					
8 a.m.					
9 a.m.					
10 a.m.					
11 a.m.					
12 p.m.					
1 p.m.					
2 p.m.					
3 p.m.					
4 p.m.					
5 p.m.					
6 p.m.					
7 p.m.					
8 p.m.					
9 p.m.					
10 p.m.					
11 p.m.					
12 a.m.					
1 a.m.					
2 a.m.					
3 a.m.					
4 a.m.					
5 a.m.					

DAY FIVE

DAY OF THE WEEK:　　　　　DATE:

HOUR	ACTIVITY	DEPRESSION/ SADNESS	ANXIETY/ IRRITABILITY	PLEASURE/ SATISFACTION	OTHER
6 a.m.					
7 a.m.					
8 a.m.					
9 a.m.					
10 a.m.					
11 a.m.					
12 p.m.					
1 p.m.					
2 p.m.					
3 p.m.					
4 p.m.					
5 p.m.					
6 p.m.					
7 p.m.					
8 p.m.					
9 p.m.					
10 p.m.					
11 p.m.					
12 a.m.					
1 a.m.					
2 a.m.					
3 a.m.					
4 a.m.					
5 a.m.					

DAY SIX

DAY OF THE WEEK: DATE:

HOUR	ACTIVITY	DEPRESSION/ SADNESS	ANXIETY/ IRRITABILITY	PLEASURE/ SATISFACTION	OTHER
6 a.m.					
7 a.m.					
8 a.m.					
9 a.m.					
10 a.m.					
11 a.m.					
12 p.m.					
1 p.m.					
2 p.m.					
3 p.m.					
4 p.m.					
5 p.m.					
6 p.m.					
7 p.m.					
8 p.m.					
9 p.m.					
10 p.m.					
11 p.m.					
12 a.m.					
1 a.m.					
2 a.m.					
3 a.m.					
4 a.m.					
5 a.m.					

DAY SEVEN

DAY OF THE WEEK: DATE:

HOUR	ACTIVITY	DEPRESSION/ SADNESS	ANXIETY/ IRRITABILITY	PLEASURE/ SATISFACTION	OTHER
6 a.m.					
7 a.m.					
8 a.m.					
9 a.m.					
10 a.m.					
11 a.m.					
12 p.m.					
1 p.m.					
2 p.m.					
3 p.m.					
4 p.m.					
5 p.m.					
6 p.m.					
7 p.m.					
8 p.m.					
9 p.m.					
10 p.m.					
11 p.m.					
12 a.m.					
1 a.m.					
2 a.m.					
3 a.m.					
4 a.m.					
5 a.m.					

Look back at your different emotional scores for various activities. Think about which activities produced the highest or lowest levels of emotional responses.

Can you see some areas that would benefit from behavioral activation? Are any of these areas surprising, or did you already know they were causing strong emotional reactions?

What brought you the biggest sense of accomplishment? There are things you do that feel good and some things that might not feel good when doing them, but still bring a sense of satisfaction or accomplishment when complete.

Review your schedule and, in the space provided, write down the days and times where you have some gaps in your current activities. This will help you fit in time to practice the goals you're about to set.

Day: .... *Time:* ....

New Behavior: ....

Day: .... *Time:* ....

New Behavior: ....

Day: .... *Time:* ....

New Behavior: ....

Day: .... *Time:* ....

New Behavior: ....

Day: .... *Time:* ....

New Behavior: ....

EXERCISE **WHERE TO BEGIN?**

You may feel like you have a lot of behaviors to change—habits to increase or decrease. Don't worry; you'll have plenty of time to work on each of them in the upcoming life domain sections. For now, you're simply going to choose a few to start with so that you can begin to practice.

List three healthy habits from your past that you'd like to restart:

1.

2.

3.

List three healthy habits from your present that you'd like to maintain:

1.

2.

3.

List one current habit you'd like to stop:

DEGREE OF DIFFICULTY

It's important to pay attention to your stress levels when working on a goal so that you maintain a moderate level. You want to be challenged—and that will involve some stress—but you don't want to feel so much stress that you give up altogether. These stress levels can include things like anxiety, fear, anger, or even physiological responses. This worksheet will help you figure out the stress level of a variety of your own experiences and use them to compare to the levels you feel as you work toward your goals.

Here is an example of how you might rate different events:

SCORE	HOW STRESS IS IMPACTING ME	MY PERSONAL EXPERIENCES
10	Most distressed, fight/flight/freeze response engaged, unable to think clearly	The traumatic event
7.5	Distressed, performance is impacted, high level of discomfort	Sitting in the middle of a crowded restaurant with no view of the exit
5	Moderately stressed, uncomfortable, but still able to think clearly and function appropriately	Being interviewed for a job
2.5	Minimal stress, able to perform well and think clearly	A moderately busy day at work when I'm focused on specific tasks and don't have any surprises or emergencies to handle
0	Completely relaxed, not worried about anything	Sitting on a beach watching the waves change color as the sun sets

Now, think about how you would rate some of your own experiences. Write down your personal experiences in the empty column so that you can rate your stress level when working toward your goals.

SCORE	HOW STRESS IS IMPACTING ME	MY PERSONAL EXPERIENCES
10	Most distressed, fight/flight/freeze response engaged, unable to think clearly	
7.5	Distressed, performance is impacted, high level of discomfort	
5	Moderately stressed, uncomfortable, but still able to think clearly and function appropriately	
2.5	Minimal stress, able to perform well and think clearly	
0	Completely relaxed, not worried about anything	

You can revisit this exercise after you have some experience practicing your new behaviors to see how far you've come. Chances are you will see your stress levels reducing in certain areas.

EXERCISE   TAKING THE FIRST STEP

Look back at the habits you identified in the exercise "Where to Begin" on page 37. Choose one habit you want to increase or decrease. Think about a simple activity you could start right now to do just that. Remember, it's best to start slowly. Don't try to tackle something that will be too challenging or difficult; you want to set yourself up for success. If you chose something that's too easy, you can always pick something more difficult next time. Here's an example to get you started:

- **Target Behavior/Goal:** Go running three days this week.
- **Expected Level of Difficulty:** 7.5
- **Potential Obstacles:** It might rain, I might have to work late, I might be too tired.
- **What Can I Do if Obstacles Arise?** I could run indoors on a treadmill. Instead of running after work, I could take a brisk walk during lunch. If I'm really tired, I could go for a shorter run.

Target Behavior/Goal:

Expected Level of Difficulty:

Potential Obstacles:

What Can I Do if Obstacles Arise?

EVALUATING YOUR PROGRESS

1. At the top of the following worksheet, write down your target behavior. If your target behavior doesn't have a set number of repetitions per week (for example, to stop repetitive checking of the locks on your front door), aim to practice a minimum of four times during the week.

2. Write down your results for each practice session on one of the rows. Review the preceding exercises if you need a reminder on how to rate your different levels.

3. Using the scale from the exercise "Degree of Difficulty" on page 38, fill in your anticipated difficulty levels and actual difficulty levels (0 = completely relaxed and at peace; 10 = most distressed, unable to think clearly, fight/flight/freeze response engaged).

4. Using the scale from the exercise "What Are You Doing Now?" on page 28, rate the levels of emotion you experienced while engaging in the behavior (0 = complete lack of the emotion; 10 = a high level of the emotion).

5. After you've completed a few practice sessions, your difficulty levels and your depression/sadness and anxiety/irritability levels should decrease, while your pleasure/satisfaction levels should begin to increase. The idea is to continue working on the same behavior/goal until you notice substantial changes in your levels. It's okay if this takes longer than one week. Just keep working at it until you notice substantial changes.

Target Behavior/Goal:

DATE PRACTICED	ANTICIPATED DIFFICULTY	ACTUAL DIFFICULTY	DEPRESSION/ SADNESS	ANXIETY/ IRRITABILITY	PLEASURE/ SATISFACTION	OTHER

Expect some bumps in the road. If it were easy to recover from PTSD, you wouldn't need any help. As you begin practicing your target behaviors, remember that you're looking for moderate challenges to target. If something is too easy, try something more difficult next time. If it's too hard, look for something a little less challenging.

It's okay if you don't get it quite right at first. As long as you keep working and don't give up, you're succeeding. If you find concrete obstacles in your way (for example, you didn't go to the gym because you couldn't find a babysitter) or if you selected an activity that turned out to challenge you in ways you didn't anticipate (for example, you couldn't run three miles and had to walk the last mile), you may need to problem-solve to find solutions. Feel free to modify your goals as you go.

After completing your target behavior repeatedly over a period of time, your levels of anticipated and actual difficulty should decrease, along with the levels of depression/sadness and anxiety/irritability you experience while engaging in the behaviors that serve your goals. Activities that were challenging should become a bit easier, and you might begin to feel a sense of mastery. Your levels of pleasure/satisfaction could rise as well. As these activities become less challenging and more satisfying, you can chalk that goal up as a success and move on to a new target behavior.

TRACK YOUR GOAL

The following handy tool will help you track your goal, any roadblocks you encounter, how you solve issues that arise, and your successful completion date for that goal.

Target Behavior/Goal:

Problems/Obstacles:

Solutions:

Modified Goal:

Date of Completion:

Congratulations! Now that you've reached your first goal, it's time to look at how PTSD is impacting your life in different areas, or life domains, and start tackling one goal at a time until you're able to enjoy life and live it according to your values.

TAKEAWAYS

- Behavioral activation can reconnect us with activities that bring increased feelings of pleasure and accomplishment.
- Behavioral activation was originally developed to treat depression, but it can help with a variety of symptoms that commonly occur in the aftermath of trauma.
- Our personal values are unique and tell us what is most important to us.
- As you become more aware of your values, you can identify specific goals you want to achieve.
- Other effective therapies for PTSD are Prolonged Exposure (PE), Cognitive-Processing Therapy (CPT), and Eye Movement Desensitization and Reprocessing (EMDR).

HOME LIFE

THE BASICS

WHETHER YOU LIVE ALONE in a tiny apartment in a big city or in a rambling farmhouse with a spouse, three kids, and a gaggle of geese out back, home is the place where most of us feel safe and at peace. Think about what home means to you. Perhaps it's where you recharge and rest so that you're at your best for work, school, or other areas of life. It doesn't matter if you have roommates, live with family, or live by yourself, trauma-related symptoms can dramatically alter your ability to function at home.

How has your home life changed since your traumatic experience? Chances are it's changed a lot more than you think. While you may recognize some of the biggest differences, you probably haven't even realized some of the less obvious ways trauma has infiltrated your personal life.

In this section, you'll thoroughly review your home life to make sure your actions match your values. You'll figure out how PTSD has impacted your closest relationships, the way you feel about your own behavior, the ways people in your life respond to you, and the way you respond in a variety of situations surrounding your life at home. You'll then begin to identify your goals, figure out how to reach them, and develop alternatives to your avoidance behaviors.

HOW IS YOUR HOME LIFE?

When John was nine years old, his uncle molested him during a family vacation. It's now 25 years later, and John has two sons of his own. His wife wants to spend their upcoming anniversary weekend at a hotel without the boys. Her brother and sister-in-law have offered to take the kids, but John feels like he's the only one who can see just how dangerous this situation is, and he refuses to go. His wife tells him he's being overprotective and that after 10 years of marriage, he should finally trust her family. He knows she's right. His in-laws are wonderful, but it's hard for him to trust anyone, especially with his children. After several arguments, he agrees to go, but only if they give the kids a cell phone so they can contact him if there's a problem.

On their first night away, they have a great time laughing and talking at dinner. He's happy to be alone with his wife and begins thinking it was ridiculous to be so nervous about the weekend. Back in their room, as they kiss, his wife slides one of her hands under his shirt and John freezes. He's suddenly overwhelmed by memories of the terrible things his uncle did to him. His heart starts racing, he can't stop shaking, and he starts sweating profusely.

His wife notices and thinks he's getting sick. He tries to sleep, but the unwanted memories keep playing through his mind, and he can't relax. When he finally falls asleep, he has a vivid nightmare of his uncle walking toward his children with a disturbing smile on his face. He calls out and thrashes in his sleep, waking his wife. He spends the rest of the night sitting up in bed, cell phone in hand, looking at it every minute or two to make sure he hasn't missed an urgent call or text from his boys.

This is a very serious example of how one man's childhood trauma can impact his home life and relationships with family members for years to come. Like John, if you suffered a childhood trauma, your current home life may be challenged in a variety of ways. If your trauma is more recent, you have probably noticed that changes in your mood and activities have created a significant disruption in your personal life. For instance, you may have previously enjoyed cooking at home for family or room-mates, but now you avoid shopping for food, have lost the motivation to cook, and retreat to your room as soon as you get home. Your home life may look very different from how it looked before the trauma occurred. It doesn't matter how long ago your trauma happened, the changes associated with trauma can impact your healthy routines and confuse or upset those around you. Habits develop over time and small changes in several areas may have created more change than you realize.

Maybe you can never completely relax or you feel more like a security guard than a member of your own family. You may have trouble keeping repetitive worries to yourself and you engage in behaviors that your loved ones find annoying or controlling. Some trauma survivors check the locks or check in on the safety of family members, over and over and over again. This can make concentration and focus difficult, if not impossible.

Our nervous systems are experts at detecting and responding to threats. However, when this system is damaged by severe or prolonged stress, it can misfire and create strong, unnecessary physiological responses. In an actual emergency, these responses are beneficial, but the rest of the time they can wreak havoc on your home and family life.

You may have stopped taking care of yourself or your living space if symptoms of depression have taken hold. Hobbies or interests you used to participate in may no longer appeal to you or require more energy than you have to give. It may be challenging to interact with your loved ones in a meaningful way, or you may feel discouraged about the future.

Intrusive thoughts are another symptom that can make it difficult for you to relax at home and are very troubling for loved ones. Terrifying nightmares can make sleep unpleasant and fitful. You may remember your nightmares or simply wake up with your pillow sweat-soaked and your heart pounding. Your bed partner may be disturbed or even afraid of you at night because you kick, hit, or call out while asleep.

Maybe you've experienced feelings of panic when trying to shop for something you need or when out for dinner. If you start expecting those symptoms to occur in particular situations, you may start to feel panicky when you even consider engaging in the activity or leaving your comfort zone. Besides episodes of acute anxiety, you may feel chronically jittery and anxious, like you drank too many cups of coffee in a short period of time.

Increased anger and irritability are also common trauma symptoms. You may have a "short fuse" and experience anger that escalates quickly. Anger can be particularly problematic when you act out aggressively or make hurtful comments. Even if you have no history of hurting others, loved ones may tell you that they feel afraid, especially if you speak in a loud voice.

If you do have a history of acting out, people you care about may avoid you altogether. Maybe you hide your anger from others, but you feel irritable or grouchy. You may be reluctant to express anger at all because you worry about hurting others. In this case, you may isolate yourself or avoid addressing problems because you fear escalating a conflict. This may seem like a good solution, but these unresolved issues can lead to intense eruptions of anger or a simmering resentment and disconnection from the people around you.

UNCOVERING TARGET BEHAVIORS

To identify specific things to change (aka, your "target behaviors"), let's look at how you're currently performing in areas that are often part of a good-quality home life. Some of the activities listed here may not be relevant to your home life or may not be part of your usual responsibilities—that's okay. You may also identify more than one area where you are experiencing a great deal of challenge or not meeting your basic responsibilities. If this is the case, you can prioritize the tasks that are currently having the most impact on your quality of life when you move on to identifying target behaviors.

Rate the following skills/activities according to this scale:
0 = N/A, 1 = Never, 2 = Almost never, 3 = Rarely, 4 = On occasion,
5 = Sometimes, 6 = Less frequently, 7 = Frequently, 8 = More frequently,
9 = Most of the time, 10 = Always

HOME LIFE SKILLS/ACTIVITIES	MY RATING
SELF-CARE	
I get dressed every day.	
I perform basic hygiene/personal grooming tasks daily.	
I get my hair cut when needed.	
I purchase new clothes when needed.	
Find your average score by dividing the total by the number of answers with a score higher than 0.	
SAFETY AND SECURITY	
I leave home to run routine errands.	
I feel safe and secure at home without exercising excessive caution.	
I'm able to be in the same room as others or alone in a room/house.	
Find your average score by dividing the total by the number of answers with a score higher than 0.	

HOME LIFE SKILLS/ACTIVITIES	MY RATING
INTERACTING WITH OTHERS	
I take care of family members requiring care (e.g., children, parents, disabled).	
I take care of my pets.	
I interact in a friendly and respectful manner with neighbors (e.g., saying hello, waving).	
I honor commitments to people I care about.	
I check in with my partner/roommate at day's end.	
I devote time to loved ones' interests or needs.	
I plan and share meals with others.	
I participate in activities with loved ones.	
I spend time in conversation with family members or roommates.	
I attend outside activities with loved ones (e.g., school plays, sporting events, work functions for significant other).	
I discuss problems/conflicts without resorting to aggression or destructive anger.	
I do something nice for someone that isn't expected (e.g., making a cup of coffee, bringing in the newspaper, doing someone's chores).	
I remember special days like birthdays, anniversaries, etc.	
I recognize/celebrate the achievements of loved ones/roommates.	
I express appreciation for the people I care about.	
Find your average score by dividing the total by the number of answers with a score higher than 0.	

(CONTINUED)

HOME LIFE SKILLS/ACTIVITIES (CONTINUED)	MY RATING
GENERAL TASKS/RESPONSIBILITIES	
I keep my home clean.	
I keep my home in good repair.	
My papers are organized.	
I pay bills on time.	
I attend to safety things (e.g., changing furnace filters, batteries in smoke detectors).	
I can follow the directions necessary to complete a project.	
I answer the front door or the phone and have voicemail set up.	
I do laundry before running out of clean underwear.	
I take care of my yard.	
I perform automotive care in a timely manner (e.g., oil changes, washes, routine maintenance).	
I go grocery shopping.	
I prepare meals.	

Find your average score by dividing the total by the number of answers that have a score higher than 0.

Look at your average score for each section:

- If you scored 1 to 3 in any section, make this area a priority when choosing your target behaviors.
- If you scored 4 to 7 in any section, target these behaviors once you've addressed any higher priority areas of concern.
- If you scored 8 to 10 in any section, you're functioning well in that area.

WHAT ARE YOUR TRIGGERS?

Have you ever taken a bite of candy or smelled something familiar on a warm summer's breeze that suddenly reminded you of a person, place, or event from your childhood? Maybe it brought to mind your favorite teacher, a place you visited every August, or a game you used to play with the other kids on your block. Whatever it is that caused that surge of pleasant emotion and memory is called a "trigger." Triggers can be things like sights, sounds, smells, and even thoughts, such as remembering anniversary dates. We respond to them with the same emotions that we felt for the original person, place, thing, or event.

Of course, triggers can also remind us of negative things, like traumatic events or someone who hurt us. These types of triggers can cause your PTSD symptoms to flare up in a flood of painful emotions and uncomfortable physiological experiences. To recover from PTSD, it's essential to figure out what triggers you. Unfortunately, uncovering your triggers isn't quite as easy as it sounds. Some of your PTSD triggers might be obvious, but others may be downright sneaky.

Think about your symptoms. Most likely, you recognize some triggers clearly and know which of your symptoms will kick in as a result. But there may be times that your symptoms rise up without warning. In these cases, it may seem like there isn't a trigger, but in reality, you probably aren't recognizing it. Triggers can be internal or external. Let's look at each of these in depth so that you can begin to identify them.

Internal and External Triggers

Harry's house caught fire in the middle of the night. He was awakened by the smoke detector and could smell smoke. Somehow, despite his terror, he managed to do everything right. He got everyone, including the cat, out of the house alive. Over the next few days, Harry shook constantly. He couldn't get it to stop. Now, two years later, if he drinks too many cups of coffee and begins to shake, Harry is overcome by intrusive thoughts of the horrifying moments he experienced inside the burning house.

Internal triggers are things like emotions, physical sensations, or memories. Other than memories, these types of triggers sometimes may not seem related to the trauma at all. Like Harry's shaking, it may be that the reason you're angry, feeling lonely, or have a racing heart has nothing to do with your traumatic experience, but your brain has linked those feelings to the feelings you experienced as a result of your traumatic event. This then activates your PTSD symptoms.

External triggers are often easier to spot. They are things like sights, sounds, or smells. For Harry, these are things like hearing the sound of sirens or an alarm, smelling smoke, or seeing flashing lights or a light that flickers like a flame. They can also be things like hearing a news story that's similar to our own traumatic experience or seeing the same thing happen to someone else (for example, if our PTSD is due to a car accident and we see a car accident while driving).

Of course, Harry could be triggered by watching a news report, movie, or TV show that involves a fire, or people who have lost their homes due to a hurricane, earthquake, or other natural disaster, or seeing a building burning in person. These triggers are direct reminders of the night Harry's house burned down. Chances are that when he encounters one, he's fully aware that his PTSD symptoms are about to engage.

As you recognize more and more of your own triggers, you'll be able to actively prepare for the moments when your symptoms flare up. You can then choose to respond in ways that will help relieve your symptoms over time. And that is a very good thing.

EXERCISE   YOUR TRIGGERS

For each of the following symptom categories, list anything you've noticed that triggers those symptoms in your home life. Keep in mind that one trigger can initiate multiple symptoms, so you may list the same trigger in more than one category. You may even want to ask loved ones or roommates to help you pinpoint any triggers they've observed.

Anxiety

_____

_____

_____

Anger

_____

_____

_____

Panic Attacks/Physiological Responses

Depression

Flashbacks and Intrusive Thoughts

Nightmares

Being aware of your triggers can help you put a plan in place to head them off before your symptoms become unmanageable.

Using Healthy Distraction to Get Through a Crisis

We've talked a lot about the symptoms of PTSD and how to identify them. You've learned how to set goals and plot the necessary steps to change your behavior and improve your symptoms. Now let's focus on what you can do when you're overcome by intrusive memories or feelings of panic. Like everything else, effectively using these tools will take practice, but once you know the proper way to wield them, they can stop your overwhelming symptoms in their tracks.

Bringing your attention to the present moment by using a set of techniques that help manage your PTSD is called grounding. It's simply a way to distract yourself so that your symptoms become manageable again and you make it through the crisis or stressful situation.

Think of your brain as a radio tuner. When tuned in to a station, you can't receive any other stations. Just like the radio, you can only focus on one thing at a time. Use this to your advantage. When your heart starts racing, if you feel like you can't breathe, or if a memory from your traumatic event is stuck on repeat in your brain, these strategies can help refocus your attention away from what is distressing you and into the present moment. These strategies are a type of mindfulness, and they are a simple way to ground yourself when you're feeling overwhelmed.

Look at the grounding ideas shared here and experiment with them when you're feeling calm. You don't need to use all of them. Choose a few that you think might work for you and practice them regularly. Then, the next time you're in a stressful situation, you can use them to help regain focus. By practicing several different options, you'll have the ability to move from one to another if one doesn't work when you need it to.

When practicing, it's important to go into as much detail as possible. Panic attacks and intrusive thoughts are overwhelming and demand a lot of attention. When you're experiencing them, you really need to focus on your present surroundings to retune your brain. It will be easier if you are used to practicing with a high level of detail.

Here are some ideas for grounding:

- Tune in to your immediate surroundings with your senses. Focus on as much detail as possible. Ask yourself:

  What do I see? Look around you and list everything you see: "I see a green chair, a book on the table, two tennis shoes on the floor, brown carpet, a bird in the tree . . . "

  What do I hear? Listen to the sounds in your environment and label them: "I hear a clock ticking, traffic outside, a teakettle whistling, my daughter talking, the electronic hum of my computer . . . "

  What do I smell? Try to distinguish all of the different things you can smell. If you're at home, you could go into the kitchen and open up jars of herbs and spices and focus on the smell of each.

  What do I feel? Touch the things around you, focusing on different textures. Label each one (smooth, rough, silky, porous, soft, hard, springy, etc.).

- Choose a task that requires mental focus. For example:

  - Count backward from 100 by threes.

  - Move through the alphabet naming a sports team or country for each letter.

- Drink a cup of coffee or tea. Focus on the scent, temperature, and taste. Notice how it feels in your mouth as the warm liquid travels down your throat.

- Carry a comforting object to touch (a pebble from your favorite beach, a sobriety token, your wedding ring, etc.).

- Create an electronic collection of soothing items on your phone so you always have something to focus on when triggered (photos of loved ones, favorite songs, funny memes, etc.).

- Take a warm or cool shower.

- Balance on one foot or try another activity that requires focused attention.

- Scan your body and notice how it feels. Notice the pace of your breathing and the way your chest moves up and down. Practice slowing the pace of your breath with your attention. Breathe in for a count of 5, out for a count of 10.

Grounding is a healthy, but temporary, strategy that you can use to get through stressful situations. When used in conjunction with the other strategies you've learned, like getting active and exposing yourself to uncomfortable situations, your PTSD tool kit will be that much more effective.

WHAT ARE YOUR AVOIDANCE BEHAVIORS?

Manuel was in a car accident that resulted in the death of his best friend. Before the accident, he enjoyed driving and was comfortable as a passenger. Now he's completely unwilling to be a passenger or drive on the freeway, schedules all car trips during low-traffic times, and drives out of his way to avoid the road where the accident occurred.

Last week, he got stuck in an unexpected traffic jam. He was so overwhelmed with anxiety that he worried he would get into another accident. He pulled over and walked home, asking his brother to return for the car. He constantly fears getting into an accident that will result in someone being injured. He used to enjoy driving his mom and her two neighbors to do their weekly shopping, but now he gets so nervous in the crowded parking lot and with the noise of everyone talking in the car that he's asked his brother to do it instead.

Traumatic events are powerful learning experiences. Our instinct for survival motivates us to avoid situations that have harmed us in the past. When our brain senses the possibility of danger, we experience a wave of uncomfortable thoughts and feelings coupled with the natural urge to stay away from whatever is causing us distress.

As we discussed earlier, a fight, flight, or freeze response that has been damaged by trauma is subject to false alarms. When our triggers cause these false alarms, we react with avoidance, escape, or safety behaviors. If these behaviors bring relief from our intense discomfort, it can be incredibly reinforcing, which makes us more likely to engage in the avoidance behavior again in the future. Even though these behaviors may look different on the surface, they all serve the same function of bringing us temporary relief from a perceived danger.

Maybe you're aware of things you actively avoid that remind you of the trauma, like people, places, or things, but avoidance can also impact you in more subtle ways like waiting in the car while your partner does the grocery shopping, buying your groceries late at night while the store is empty, or running in to grab what you need as quickly as possible. Isolation may have snuck up on you. Maybe you've started spending an increasing amount of time in a room by yourself, avoiding common areas and the people you live with.

Another form of avoidance is to use substances like alcohol to manage your anxiety when family members or friends visit your home, or you feel like you need to drink or get high to unwind at the end of the day. Substance use is a type of avoidance because it allows you to go into a situation and avoid actually experiencing it, or it allows you to escape from painful memories and emotional reactions.

Friends or family may offer support by asking about your experience, but you avoid talking or even thinking about your trauma. Your behavior may confuse your significant other, and they may even feel shut out by your refusal to share your feelings. They may also have difficulty understanding why some situations are so uncomfortable that you feel an intense need to escape or avoid them altogether. This may be complicated by the fact that you may not entirely understand your own reactions and triggers. In the past, you may have enjoyed family gatherings and now you stand alone in a corner and leave as soon as possible, or just stay home while the rest of your family attends.

Escape behaviors are just what they sound like. You use escape to get out of a stressful situation. Perhaps you go work out in the garage if your kids have a bunch of friends over, or you leave the house if you and your spouse get into an argument.

Then there are safety behaviors. When we talk about safety behaviors, we don't want you to think that being safe is a bad thing. Of course, it's smart to lock your front door at night, pay attention to your surroundings when walking in a big city, or monitor your toddler's whereabouts to make sure they don't climb the nearest bookcase. The types of safety behaviors we're talking about here are extreme and excessive behaviors that you use to cope with your symptoms. These may include things like repeatedly checking locks, refusing to let your child play at another child's home, or carrying a weapon with you at all times, even if you are just going to use the bathroom for a few minutes.

EXERCISE YOUR AVOIDANCE BEHAVIORS

Contemplate the avoidance behaviors you use in your home life. In this worksheet, list your avoidance behaviors in the first column. In the second column, identify the situations in which you use those behaviors to cope.

AVOIDANCE BEHAVIOR	I USE THIS BEHAVIOR WHEN . . .

HOW IS AVOIDANCE WORKING FOR YOU?

Avoidance behaviors develop over time, and we stick with them because they bring us some kind of short-term gain. Think about the coping strategies you just identified that you use to face challenges in your daily life. If they didn't have some positive impact, you would have abandoned them long ago. Of course, these behaviors also have many negative effects. For example, maybe you deal with your anxiety by repeatedly checking on the safety of your loved ones via text. Chances are that you try to hide your true intentions by camouflaging these safety checks as something else, like "I love you!" or "Hope you're having a good day!" When your loved ones respond quickly, you're rewarded with the relief of knowing they're okay. But if you don't get an immediate response, your concern for their well-being surges until you feel compelled to send rapid-fire messages begging for or demanding their response. This can make you angry or anxious, and it can be extremely frustrating for the people you care about who may feel your behavior is controlling or reflects a lack of trust.

EXERCISE   YOUR AVOIDANCE GAINS AND LOSSES

It's important to recognize the positives and negatives associated with the avoidance strategies you've been relying on in your home life. That way, you can anticipate potential challenges as you begin to change your behavior. Respond to the following prompts in the spaces provided.

Describe a situation that triggers an avoidance behavior and explain exactly how you react.

What are the payoffs for avoiding this situation?

_____

_____

_____

_____

What are the negative results of avoiding this situation?

_____

_____

_____

_____

WHAT ARE YOUR ALTERNATIVES?

Now that you're aware of some of the consequences of the behaviors you use to cope with stress, it's time to consider alternatives that will bring your behavior more in line with your values.

Anxiety is uncomfortable. Until now it may have seemed like your only alternative was to escape or avoid that discomfort. When our brain sends powerful messages like, "I need to get out of here now!" it may feel more like a command than a suggestion. However, you do have the ability to choose an alternative behavior that aligns with your values and target behaviors.

Although it's normal to feel this way, don't get discouraged about how far your current behavior is from where you'd like it to be. Try taking on complex or challenging tasks by breaking them down into smaller parts. As you master these basic steps, your confidence will grow and you'll be ready to tackle greater challenges.

Pay attention to your successful coping strategies already in place so you can apply them in areas where you're still struggling. For example, if you're able to calm down by taking a short time-out when feeling frustrated with your two-year-old, you could try the same approach when negotiating a conflict with the contractor repairing your septic tank.

EXERCISE YOUR ALTERNATIVES

Review the avoidance behaviors you identified in the exercise "Your Avoidance Behaviors" on page 55 that have negative consequences in your home life. It's time to consider your alternatives. Respond to the following prompts in the spaces provided.

Think about the negative consequences or costs of your avoidance behaviors. How do they interfere with your long-term goals?

(For example: I check the door and windows repeatedly to make sure they're locked. I insist that the people I live with recheck the locks of any doors they've opened and they've said they find this demand unreasonable. When I wake up in the middle of the night, I get up to check that everything is locked and I disturb my bed partner and find it more difficult to fall back to sleep.)

What could you try instead? List three to five options for alternative responses.

(For example: I can agree to refrain from asking the people I live with to recheck the locks. When I wake up at night, I can remind myself that I checked the locks before going to bed. I can reassure myself that I'm safe and that feeling anxious doesn't mean I'm in danger.)

BREAKING DOWN TARGET BEHAVIORS

Refer back to the challenge areas you identified in the exercise "Uncovering Target Behaviors" on page 46. Choose a behavior to target. Every time you practice your target behavior, you will be building a new habit.

In this exercise, you'll identify some smaller goals or steps you can take to increase your chance of success. Some of these steps may be uncomfortable and require multiple repetitions before you're ready to move on to the next step. Fill in all of your anticipated difficulty ratings now, before you even begin to practice them. It's okay if some of your numbers are very high—they will decrease as you practice.

If one of your steps involves doing the activity with someone you know, it's a good idea to explain what you're doing before you start. This will help them understand your behavior if you get uncomfortable and make it easier for you to stay on track.

Here's an example to get you started:

Target Behavior: Attend outside activities with loved ones.

Specific Goal: Attend the annual neighborhood block party with my loved ones.

STEPS I CAN TAKE RIGHT NOW TO REACH MY GOAL	ANTICIPATED DIFFICULTY 0 = easy, 5 = moderately uncomfortable, 10 = impossible
When I see a neighbor outside, do not immediately rush away.	4
Make eye contact and wave when I see them, say hello from a distance.	4
Take short walks around my neighborhood, engage in short and friendly conversations when possible (talk about the weather, how nice their house looks, their new car, etc.).	5
Take longer walks around the neighborhood, initiate contact with any neighbors I encounter.	6
Attend the annual event and meet any guidelines I've established (a minimum amount of time I want to stay, talking to a certain number of different people, eating a full plate of food, participating in one game, not drinking alcohol to alleviate my symptoms, etc.).	7.5

Target Behavior:

Specific Goal:

STEPS I CAN TAKE RIGHT NOW TO REACH MY GOAL	ANTICIPATED DIFFICULTY 0 = easy, 5 = moderately uncomfortable, 10 = impossible

Now that you have an idea of what steps you can take toward your target behavior, identify any obstacles you might encounter and how you will overcome them so that you have a plan in place.

What obstacles might prevent you from practicing?

(For example: I work the night shift and rarely see my neighbors.)

How can you overcome these obstacles?

(For example: I can make extra effort on the weekends when I'm off work.)

ACTION PLAN FOR CHANGE

It's time to create an action plan to help you strategize and make key decisions about how you'll respond *before* a triggering situation arises in your home life. That way you'll have a plan in place when the time comes to make choices about trying new alternatives. Some new behaviors will be immediately rewarding, such as spending more time with your kids, but others will take some time to demonstrate their benefits. To identify appropriate goals, consider your values (you will do this in the first step).

Values are important because they remind us of the direction we want to move in. After determining which direction you want to go, focus on identifying a moderately challenging goal and the type of reinforcement you'll need to stay motivated.

Consider creating a reward system for practicing, particularly for behaviors where it might take longer for you to get the full benefit of the natural reinforcement. Rewards should be something you look forward to, like watching a show after each practice session or spending 15 minutes relaxing in the hammock in your backyard. If you enjoy music, you could purchase one new album or song after successfully completing a step or a goal. Figure out what will motivate you to keep moving forward, even when things get challenging.

STEP ONE

In section 2, you identified your top three values (see page 27). Reflect on these values and consider how they apply to your home life. Ultimately, multiple values will come into play, but for now, start with one you think is most important for this area and write it in the space provided.

Value: ....

STEP TWO

Think of a target behavior that relates to that value and identify your specific goal. Write them in the spaces provided. Remember, if your target behavior doesn't have a set number of repetitions, try to practice a minimum of four times during the next week.

Target Behavior: ....

Specific Goal: ....

STEP THREE

What problems or obstacles do you think you might encounter as you work toward your goal?

Problems/Obstacles:

STEP FOUR

What solutions or modifications can you try if problems or obstacles arise?

Solutions/Modifications:

STEP FIVE

What avoidance behaviors do you think you might want to participate in as you challenge yourself?

Potential Avoidance Behaviors:

STEP SIX

What can you try instead of the avoidance behaviors?

Alternatives to Avoidance Behaviors:

STEP SEVEN

What will reinforce your new behavior? What desirable things will naturally occur as a result of trying the new behavior that will be enjoyable to you? These are the things that will keep you moving forward.

My Behavior Reinforcement:

STEP EIGHT

Review the exercise "Breaking Down Target Behaviors" on page 60. In the space provided, write down the steps you can take to work up to your ultimate goal. These steps will help you identify new behaviors to target as you achieve mastery of your initial target behaviors.

Steps to Take:

1.

2.

3.

4.

STEP NINE

When you reach your goal or complete your target behavior, what type of reward do you expect to receive? This may be a personal sense of accomplishment or satisfaction or some external reward like the thanks of a loved one.

Rewards for Success:

STEP TEN

In the following worksheet, record the results from your practice sessions. If necessary, review the exercise "Evaluating Your Progress" on page 40.

1. Record the date of each practice session.
2. Using the scale from the exercise "Degree of Difficulty" on page 38, fill in your anticipated difficulty levels and actual difficulty levels (0 = completely relaxed and at peace; 10 = most distressed, unable to think clearly, fight/flight/freeze response engaged).
3. Using the scale from the exercise "What Are You Doing Now?" on page 28, rate the levels of emotion you experienced while practicing the behavior (0 = complete lack of the emotion; 10 = a high level of the emotion).
4. After you've completed a few practice sessions, your difficulty levels and your depression/sadness and anxiety/irritability levels should decrease, while your pleasure/satisfaction levels should gradually increase. The idea is to continue working on the same target behavior until you notice substantial changes in your levels. It's okay if this takes longer than one week. Some very challenging behaviors may take several weeks to become more comfortable. Just keep working at it until you notice substantial changes. When one step becomes less challenging, you'll be ready to move on to the next step toward your goal.

DATE PRACTICED	ANTICIPATED DIFFICULTY (0–10)	ACTUAL DIFFICULTY (0–10)	DEPRESSION/ SADNESS (0–10)	ANXIETY/ IRRITABILITY (0–10)	PLEASURE/ SATISFACTION (0–10)	OTHER (0–10)

STEP ELEVEN

Once you've reached your goal, assess what went well and what didn't. Use that information to help decide which behavior to target next.

Next Target Behavior:

YOUR HOME LIFE ACTION PLAN

Now let's take all the information you've gathered on your target behaviors, potential obstacles, and rewards and create an action plan for your first home life goal.

Target Behavior:

Specific Goal:

Problems/Obstacles:

Solutions/Modifications:

Potential Avoidance Behaviors:

Alternatives to Avoidance Behaviors:

Behavior Reinforcement:

Steps to Take:

1.

2.

3.

4.

5.

Anticipated Rewards for Success:

DATE PRACTICED	ANTICIPATED DIFFICULTY (0–10)	ACTUAL DIFFICULTY (0–10)	DEPRESSION/ SADNESS (0–10)	ANXIETY/ IRRITABILITY (0–10)	PLEASURE/ SATISFACTION (0–10)	OTHER (0–10)

Next Target Behavior:

REVIEWING YOUR PROGRESS

Now that you've set an initial goal for your home life and practiced your target behavior, let's assess your progress. Respond to the following prompts in the spaces provided:

How did you feel when you completed this goal?

_____

_____

_____

Were there any unexpected challenges? If so, what were they?

_____

_____

_____

Was anything easier than expected?

_____

_____

_____

How did you overcome the obstacles you encountered?

_____

_____

_____

Should you try to take on a less challenging task next time, or are you ready to increase the intensity?

How difficult will it be to maintain your new behavior?

How can you overcome obstacles that could interfere with engaging in this behavior in the future?

TAKEAWAYS

- Trauma-related symptoms can have a dramatic impact on your home life.
- You may experience anxiety, avoidance, intrusive memories, panic attacks, anger, and depression that make functioning in this area very difficult.
- Triggers are reminders of things that happened to us in the past, and we respond to them with the same emotions we felt toward the original experience.
- Healthy distraction can help you get through a crisis.
- Avoidance behaviors can help you cope with stress in your home life, but they can keep you from moving toward your values and achieving your goals.

WORK LIFE

THE BASICS

Think about what your professional life means to you. Perhaps you work in an office, on a construction site, or in a restaurant. Maybe you're a university student, a trade apprentice, or you volunteer your time and energy for a nonprofit organization or at your local library. You may be currently out of work and reviewing your options as you plot the next step forward in your career. You may work full time, part time, or on an occasional, contract basis. Maybe you work all day and take classes at night.

Whatever your professional life looks like, the time you spend pursuing it should be a source of pride and self-satisfaction. When the symptoms of PTSD interfere with this important life domain, your confidence can take a hit. And as self-doubt takes hold, your symptoms can increase and disrupt your ability to succeed in your chosen vocation.

How has your work life been impacted by your traumatic experience? If your trauma is recent, how you operate at work has probably changed more than you realize. You may recognize some of the biggest differences or challenges you face, but you may not be aware of some of the less obvious ways trauma has infiltrated your professional life.

In this section, you'll review your work life to make sure your actions match your values and are moving you in the direction you want to go. You'll look at the ways PTSD has impacted relationships with your peers and managers, how you feel about your own behavior, the ways your coworkers and other people in your work environment respond to you, and the way you respond in a variety of situations. You'll then identify your goals, figure out how to reach them, and work on developing alternatives to your avoidance behaviors.

HOW IS YOUR WORK LIFE?

In the previous section, we introduced you to John (see page 44). Just because John's experience of being sexually abused as a child was directly related to his home life doesn't mean that other areas of his life are symptom-free. Not only is he easily distracted from his job if his wife or sons don't check in with him when they're supposed to, but anything unexpected or unresolved causes a chain reaction of anxiety and insecurity.

One of John's PTSD symptoms is a hyperawareness of the moods and habits of others. Last week at work, he noticed that the managers were distracted and distant. Normally they engage in conversation and smile as they pass him in the hall. On Monday, when John realized that they were also having a large number of closed-door meetings, he began to worry. What if the company was in financial trouble? Or what if they were unhappy with his work? Was he going to be laid off or disciplined? John's anxiety grew exponentially over the next few days. His stomach was upset, and he felt on edge and irritable. He couldn't focus on tasks and even forgot to attend an important meeting that he had organized. On Wednesday, one of John's favorite coworkers asked him to help with a last-minute project. He snapped at her and said he was much too busy to do her work as well as his own.

On Thursday afternoon, an all-office meeting was announced for the following morning. John couldn't sleep that night, convinced that the news was terrible. How was he going to support his family without a job? He was full of dread as he walked into the conference room for the meeting. But when the meeting began, he realized that the managers who'd been so preoccupied all week were laughing and smiling at everyone. Instead of bad news, they shared details of an exciting new opportunity that had taken weeks to negotiate. John's worries evaporated. Because of PTSD, he'd spent the whole week in a continuous state of anxiety, irritability, and pessimism.

This is an example of how one man's trauma affected his work life and professional relationships. It's been a very long time since John was assaulted. He may not even realize that some of his feelings and behaviors are a direct result of his trauma. Now let's look at some of the other ways the PTSD symptoms you learned about in section 1 might be impacting you professionally.

Symptoms of anxiety can be a major obstacle in your work life. Hypervigilance, the feeling of being chronically on guard, makes it difficult to accomplish anything. Startle responses to sudden loud noises or movements can bring unwanted attention, particularly if you haven't shared your trauma history with coworkers. It can be difficult to concentrate or focus, especially if the environment isn't comfortable for you. Doubting yourself or feeling the need to double-check your work or the safety of your workplace can hurt your performance and make it difficult to complete assignments.

In addition, a depressed mood can make it hard to find the energy, interest, and motivation to do anything. You may lack the confidence you used to have, which often increases the negative judgments you make about yourself. It can even make you feel like others are also making negative judgments about you. This cycle makes it hard to identify your goals, complete tasks, and meet your responsibilities on a daily basis.

Sometimes, in an effort to protect us from danger, our brains respond to safe stimuli as if they're threatening. This process happens quickly and without any conscious thought, so that we don't have time to think about what we're seeing, hearing, or smelling—we simply act. When something reminds us of danger, a fight, flight, or freeze response is triggered. In an actual emergency, this immediate response can save our life, but in a harmless, professional setting it can be very disorienting, uncomfortable, or embarrassing.

And, of course, anger can cause significant challenges in the workplace. You may struggle to address concerns without offending others or they may complain that you're angry, even when you're not. Even if you avoid outbursts, you may be irritable and easily annoyed by people or situations that don't meet your expectations.

UNCOVERING TARGET BEHAVIORS

To identify specific goals, let's look at how you're performing the tasks that are often part of a good-quality work life. Some of the activities listed may not be relevant to your work life or may not be part of your usual responsibilities—that's okay. You may also identify more than one area where you are experiencing a great deal of challenge or not meeting your basic responsibilities. If this is the case, you can prioritize the tasks that are currently having the most impact on your quality of life when you move on to identifying target behaviors.

Rate the following skills/activities according to this scale:
0 = N/A, 1 = Never, 2 = Almost never, 3 = Rarely, 4 = On occasion,
5 = Sometimes, 6 = Less frequently, 7 = Frequently, 8 = More frequently,
9 = Most of the time, 10 = Always

WORK LIFE SKILLS/ACTIVITIES	MY RATINGS
SELF-CARE	
I've identified vocational goals (e.g., financially supporting my family, working more hours, going to school).	
I go after opportunities that I want (e.g., applying for a job/promotion, initiating volunteer work, signing up for classes).	
I follow through on commitments (e.g., attend class, complete school/work assignments, meet volunteer commitments).	
I learn new skills for my chosen vocation/education.	
I have long-term plans or vocational goals.	
Find your average score by dividing the total by the number of answers with a score higher than 0.	
SAFETY AND SECURITY	
I feel safe and secure at work without exercising excessive caution.	
I'm able to be in the same room as others or alone in the office and not worry about my safety.	
Find your average score by dividing the total by the number of answers with a score higher than 0.	

(CONTINUED)

WORK LIFE SKILLS/ACTIVITIES (CONTINUED)	MY RATINGS
INTERACTING WITH OTHERS	
I maintain friendly or cordial relationships with coworkers/classmates.	
I'm able to take direction from superiors or teachers.	
I'm able to maintain constructive feedback/address concerns about others' work habits/performance without resorting to destructive anger.	
I'm able to work effectively in a group/on a team.	
I communicate with others in a reasonable way about things that are triggering for me.	
I'm able to accept criticism/feedback about my work.	
I interact appropriately with customers, service providers, and fellow students.	
I can share a workspace with others or be alone.	
Find your average score by dividing the total by the number of answers with a score higher than 0.	
GENERAL TASKS/RESPONSIBILITIES	
I'm prompt to work and meetings.	
I only call in sick when physically ill.	
I maintain a neat and orderly workspace.	
I retain and process information that I read.	
I'm able to file necessary paperwork for school, financial aid, disability, business license, etc.	
I can follow directions.	
I'm able to maintain focus and concentration on a project.	

GENERAL TASKS/RESPONSIBILITIES (CONTINUED)	MY RATINGS
I'm able to take on and complete challenging and complicated projects.	
I can cope with interruptions or deal with unexpected tasks.	
I can cope with stressful or unexpected situations.	
Find your average score by dividing the total by the number of answers that have a score higher than 0.	

Look at your average score for each section:

- If you scored 1 to 3 in any section, make this area a priority when choosing your target behaviors.
- If you scored 4 to 7 in any section, target these behaviors once you've addressed any higher priority areas of concern.
- If you scored 8 to 10 in any section, you're functioning well in that area.

WHAT ARE YOUR TRIGGERS?

In section 3, we introduced triggers and provided a thorough explanation of what they are and how they affect you and your PTSD symptoms. If you're taking the life domains out of order and haven't read section 3 yet, turn to page 49 and read about triggers. It's essential that you understand what they are so that you can identify your own triggers in the next exercise.

> Luis has always loved rebuilding classic cars. After working in the same auto shop for years, he was called up as an Army Reservist and served as a mechanic in a combat zone. Returning to his former life has been more of a challenge than he expected. Before he was deployed, Luis loved going to work each day, telling the same jokes with the same group of coworkers, who were also his friends. He loved the challenge of taking an old, beat-up car and bringing it back to life one piece at a time. He was the one the guys came to when they couldn't find a fix for a puzzling mechanical issue. He was proud that his calm, patient, methodical approach always discovered the solution. When he returned from deployment, he was welcomed back with open arms, but he soon began to wonder if he should find a new job.

Concentration Practice

Trauma survivors often struggle with concentration and focus. If this sounds familiar, you may have given up doing activities that require your full attention. To recover the ability to fully focus on one thing at a time and rediscover the activities you've abandoned, you need to exercise your ability to concentrate. With time and practice, your ability to maintain your concentration and focus will improve.

Think about a time when you were working on a project or participating in an activity that required so much concentration that you couldn't think about anything except what you were doing from one moment to the next. Maybe you looked up after hours had gone by, and you hadn't even realized it because you were so focused on what you were doing. As mentioned in the previous section, when we focus on one thing in the present moment, it's called mindfulness. Although it's natural and satisfying for us to focus on one thing at a time, in a modern, digital world we're continuously bombarded with different sources of stimulation that make it difficult to fully engage in the moment.

When you're ready to practice awareness of the present, select some of the following activities or choose another activity to practice with your full attention. That may sound simple, but you'll soon discover that it's not always easy to keep your mind from wandering. As you practice, pay attention to what you're doing, your thoughts, and your feelings, without judging them or trying to change them.

If you notice something unpleasant or uncomfortable, try not to push it away. At the same time, if you notice something pleasant or enjoyable, try not to hang on to it a bit longer. Simply observe your experience and do your best not to force any type of change. If you realize you've become distracted, just bring your attention back to the present and your task at hand. Like any skill, the more you practice, the easier it will be for you to stay in the moment.

Here are some effective activities for mindfulness practice:

- Walking slowly while paying attention to what you see, hear, feel, and smell

- Practicing a skillful physical activity like martial arts, yoga, or improving your golf or tennis swing

- Focusing completely on a mental task, such as filing and doing detailed paperwork

- Focusing completely on a physical task that requires skill, such as operating machinery or repairing equipment

- Playing games of skill like pool or darts

- Eating silently while focusing on the colors, smells, tastes, and textures of the food

- Practicing a musical instrument

- Doing crafts such as woodworking, ceramics, or painting

- Enjoying nature by watching a sunrise or sunset or listening to waves breaking on the beach or the sound of wind rustling through the trees

- Taking a mindful break, such as going for a short walk or sitting quietly while paying attention to your feelings and surroundings

- Doing yard work such as mowing, planting, raking, or weeding

- Praying

- Meditating

He now dreads going to work each day. The metallic, grease-heavy smell of the garage often makes him feel flushed, light-headed, and unable to breathe. He has to take frequent breaks to walk around outside until his head clears. Time and again, when a coworker drops something heavy like a wrench or if someone uses a pneumatic tool when he's not expecting it, Luis jumps, his heart racing and adrenaline flooding his system. His coworkers have made comments about it so he tries to play it off as a joke every time it happens. His muscles are constantly tense. He can no longer relax because he's so nervous that something is going to startle him.

Luis worries that he's losing his mind. He forgets things and can't concentrate on what he's doing long enough to puzzle through the same sorts of mechanical challenges he used to relish. His patience is gone. Last week, he became so frustrated when he couldn't fix something that he threw the part across the shop. When one of the guys came over and put his arm over his shoulder to see if he was okay, Luis yelled at him and pushed him away.

In this example of work-related triggers, Luis reacts to an *internal trigger* when he gets angry and can't find the solution to a challenge. Memories of the traumatic event are obvious *internal triggers*, but they can also be things like physical sensations (heart racing, muscle tension, shaking from too much caffeine, etc.) that aren't directly related to your trauma. They can also be things like emotions. Maybe you've had an argument with someone that had nothing to do with your traumatic experience, but the situationally appropriate emotions you were feeling in that moment caused your PTSD symptoms to activate. If this happens to you, it means that your brain has linked those feelings and emotions to your traumatic experience.

For most of us, *external triggers*—things we see, hear, or smell—are the easiest to recognize. For Luis, these are loud, unexpected sounds; the smells of oil, grease, and metallic auto parts; or seeing the banged-up, twisted parts of a damaged car. They can also be any unexpected war references when he's watching a news report, movie, or TV show, or if he reads news online. These triggers are direct reminders of his combat experience, and, when he encounters one, he knows his PTSD symptoms are about to kick in.

As you figure out what your own triggers are, you can start to prepare for a flare-up of symptoms and choose how you'll respond to them. Over time, this will help reduce your symptoms and get you back to living the life you want to lead.

YOUR TRIGGERS

For each of the following symptom categories, list anything you've noticed that triggers those symptoms in your work life. Keep in mind that one trigger can initiate multiple symptoms, so you may list the same trigger in more than one category. You may even want to ask trusted friends or coworkers to help you pinpoint any triggers they've observed.

Anxiety

Anger

Panic Attacks/Physiological Responses

Depression

Flashbacks and Intrusive Thoughts

Nightmares

Being aware of your triggers can help you put a plan in place to head them off before your symptoms become unmanageable.

Resolving Conflict the Healthy Way

Conflict is inevitable, and conflicts at work can be particularly tricky to navigate. We each have unique wants, needs, thoughts, and feelings. When we interact with others, differences of opinion are bound to come up and can become an issue if we're unable to communicate our desires in a healthy way. Problems occur when we try to force others to see our point of view, but we're just as likely to fail if we fear conflict and, therefore, avoid addressing our concerns at all.

As you navigate the process of conflict resolution, look at the basic types of communication discussed here, figure out which you use during a conflict, and think about how they might be impacting your interactions with others. Assertive communication is the healthiest way to communicate, so we'll start with that one.

Assertive communication—You ask directly for what you want or need while also paying attention to the rights and needs of others. You clearly communicate your thoughts or feelings while avoiding harsh criticism or emotional attacks. Signs of assertive communication are maintaining eye contact, using a calm voice, and listening to the responses of others.

Passive communication—You actively avoid expressing your thoughts or feelings to avoid conflict. It also prevents you from indicating your own wants or needs. Signs of passive communication include being inappropriately apologetic or accepting an unwanted outcome without stating your position.

Aggressive communication—You advocate for your own point of view at the expense of others. This type of communication is frequently perceived as bullying and may be prompted by a feeling of powerlessness. Signs that communication has become aggressive include raising your voice, talking over others, and direct or indirect threats.

Passive-aggressive communication—While this may look passive, it's actually a subtle way to communicate hostility. You may use it in an effort to reveal your anger while avoiding direct confrontation. It involves being outwardly cooperative, while using subtle put-downs or sabotage. Signs of passive-aggressive communication include indirectly undermining others, mumbling or speaking under your breath, and smiling while offering false agreement. You're using passive-aggressive communication if you agree with someone in a superficially pleasant manner, but then set disagreeable conditions or complete the task in an unpleasant manner. You may use this type of communication style when you no longer think you can resolve a conflict in a straightforward manner.

Reread the description of assertive communication. If communication is a challenge for you, perhaps this is a behavior you'd like to target in your work life, or any of your life domains.

WHAT ARE YOUR AVOIDANCE BEHAVIORS?

Rajesh is an experienced public defender. His coworkers are not aware that he's a trauma survivor, and he works hard to maintain his image as a competent professional. Most of the time, he's able to manage his symptoms, but certain cases trigger memories of his own personal trauma history. Sometimes when he fears a case may trigger him, he delegates it to his junior colleagues. He's called in sick multiple times, and others have had to cover for him in court.

As we discussed in the previous section, after a traumatic experience, your damaged fight, flight, or freeze response is subject to false alarms. (If you need a refresher of this important information, see page 3.) Avoidance comes up in your professional life in a variety of ways. Like Rajesh, you may rely on avoidance to manage your reactions to situations that trigger trauma-related responses. You may actively avoid particular sights, sounds, smells, or topics that trigger your symptoms.

Avoidance can also show up in more subtle ways. Perhaps you spend most of your time alone in your office and only interact with others when you have to. You may rely on alcohol or prescription or nonprescription drugs before, during, or after professional activities to manage stress. You may use safety behaviors such as selecting a desk close to an exit or maintaining access to some sort of weapon in case of danger. And, finally, if you've ever made up an excuse to step out of a meeting, perhaps to use the bathroom or grab something you forgot, then you've used escape as a way to reduce your symptoms.

YOUR AVOIDANCE BEHAVIORS

Contemplate the avoidance behaviors you use in your work life. In this worksheet, list your avoidance behaviors in the first column. In the second column, identify the situations in which you use those behaviors to cope.

AVOIDANCE BEHAVIOR	I USE THIS BEHAVIOR WHEN . . .

HOW IS AVOIDANCE WORKING FOR YOU?

In the previous exercise, you identified some of the coping strategies you use to face challenges in your professional life. Obviously, the avoidance behaviors you've developed over time work for you in some way, or you wouldn't continue using them. Maybe you prevent panic attacks or physiological responses by avoiding a task that reminds you of your traumatic event. If the task isn't essential to your job, maybe it's no big deal, at least in the short term. However, if the task you're avoiding is required or otherwise important to job performance, avoiding it may help you avoid panic attacks, but it can cause significant problems in other ways.

YOUR AVOIDANCE GAINS AND LOSSES

It's important to recognize the positives and negatives associated with the avoidance strategies you've been relying on in your work life. That way, you can anticipate potential challenges as you begin to change your behavior. Respond to the following prompts in the spaces provided.

Describe a work situation that triggers an avoidance behavior and explain exactly how you react.

_____

_____

_____

_____

What are the payoffs for avoiding this situation?

_____

_____

_____

_____

What are the negative results of avoiding this situation?

_____

_____

_____

_____

WHAT ARE YOUR ALTERNATIVES?

Being aware of how you cope with stress is the first step to bringing your behavior in line with your values so you can get out and live your life again. Now let's look for alternatives to your avoidance behaviors. Don't be discouraged about how far your current behavior is from where you want it to be. If you take difficult tasks one small step at a time, you'll make progress and your confidence will grow as you prepare to take on bigger challenges.

Think about successful coping strategies already in place to see if you can use them for other problem areas. For example, try applying constructive communication skills that you've practiced with your partner to help resolve conflicts with your boss.

If you're reading the life domains out of order, please go back to page 58 in section 3 for more detailed information on this topic before moving on to the following exercise.

YOUR ALTERNATIVES

Review the avoidance behaviors you identified on page 82, and consider your alternatives to the ones that have negative consequences in your work life. Respond to the following prompts in the spaces provided.

Think about the negative consequences or costs of your avoidance behaviors. How do they interfere with your long-term goals?

(For example: It's hard for me to be in a room with more than one or two other people for more than a few minutes, so I pretend I forgot there was a meeting, or that something important came up, and show up toward the end. I'm good at my job and want to be promoted someday, but I've been reprimanded for missing so many meetings.)

What could you try instead? List three to five options for alternative responses.

(For example: During a meeting, I can practice healthy distraction exercises. I can also focus on what is being discussed instead of the people who are surrounding me.)

Refer back to the challenge areas you identified in the exercise "Uncovering Target Behaviors" on page 73. Choose a behavior to target. Every time you practice your target behavior, you will be building a new habit.

In this exercise, you'll identify some smaller goals or steps you can take to increase your chances of success. Some of these steps may be uncomfortable and require multiple repetitions before you're ready to move on to the next step. Fill in all of your anticipated difficulty ratings now, before you even begin to practice them. It's okay if some of your numbers are very high—they will decrease as you practice.

If one of your steps involves doing the activity with someone you know, it's a good idea to explain what you're doing before you start. This will help them understand your behavior if you get uncomfortable and make it easier for you to stay on track.

Here is an example to get you started:

Target Behavior: Follow through on commitments (attend class, complete school/work assignments, meet volunteer commitments).

Specific Goal: To successfully complete a class.

STEPS I CAN TAKE RIGHT NOW TO REACH MY GOAL	ANTICIPATED DIFFICULTY 0 = easy, 5 = moderately uncomfortable, 10 = impossible
Determine which course to take and where to take it.	3
Sign up for the course.	3
Attend each course meeting on time and prepared to learn (with books, notebooks, pens, etc.).	6
Complete and turn in all assignments on time.	7

Target Behavior: ....

Specific Goal: ....

STEPS I CAN TAKE RIGHT NOW TO REACH MY GOAL	ANTICIPATED DIFFICULTY 0 = easy, 5 = moderately uncomfortable, 10 = impossible

Now that you have an idea of what steps you can take toward your target behavior, identify any obstacles you might encounter and how you will overcome them so that you have a plan in place.

What obstacles might prevent you from practicing?

(For example: I might feel too tired to go to class or do my homework.)

....

....

How can you overcome these obstacles?

(For example: I can schedule my courses and complete my homework during the time of day when I'm most likely to feel alert and rested.)

....

....

ACTION PLAN FOR CHANGE

It's time to create an action plan to help you strategize and make key decisions before a triggering situation arises in your work life. Some of the new behaviors will be immediately rewarding, such as completing your assignments on time, but others will take a while to demonstrate their benefits. To identify appropriate goals, consider your values (you will do this in the first step).

Values are important because they remind us of the direction we want to head in. After determining your direction, focus on identifying a moderately challenging goal and the type of reinforcement you'll need to stay motivated. Consider creating a reward system for practicing. This should be something you look forward to like getting up from your desk to get a cup of coffee or getting takeout from your favorite restaurant at the end of the week. Figure out what will motivate you to keep moving forward, even when things become challenging.

STEP ONE

In section 2, you identified your top three values (see page 27). Reflect on these values and consider how they apply to your work life. Ultimately, multiple values will come into play, but for now start with one you think is most important for this area and write it in the space provided.

Value:

STEP TWO

Think of a target behavior that relates to that value and identify your specific goal. Write them in the spaces provided. (Remember, if your target behavior doesn't have a set number of repetitions, try to practice a minimum of four times during the next week.)

Target Behavior:

Specific Goal:

STEP THREE

What problems or obstacles do you think you might encounter as you work toward your goal?

Problems/Obstacles:

STEP FOUR

What solutions or modifications can you try if problems or obstacles arise?

Solutions/Modifications:

STEP FIVE

What avoidance behaviors do you think you might want to participate in as you challenge yourself?

Potential Avoidance Behaviors:

STEP SIX

What can you try instead of the avoidance behaviors?

Alternatives to Avoidance Behaviors:

STEP SEVEN

What will reinforce your new behavior?

Behavior Reinforcement:

STEP EIGHT

Review the exercise "Breaking Down Target Behaviors" on page 86. In the space provided, write down the steps you can take to work up to your ultimate goal. These steps will help you identify new behaviors to target as you achieve mastery of your initial target behaviors.

Steps to Take:

1. ....

2. ....

3. ....

4. ....

5. ....

STEP NINE

When you reach your goal or complete your target behavior, what type of reward do you expect to receive? This may be a personal sense of accomplishment or satisfaction, or some external reward like the thanks of a coworker.

Rewards for Success: ....

STEP TEN

In the following worksheet, record the results from your practice sessions. If necessary, review the exercise "Evaluating Your Progress" on page 40.

1. Record the date of each practice session.
2. Using the scale from the exercise "Degree of Difficulty" on page 38, fill in your anticipated difficulty levels and actual difficulty levels (0 = completely relaxed and at peace; 10 = most distressed, unable to think clearly, fight/flight/freeze response engaged).
3. Using the scale from the exercise "What Are You Doing Now?" on page 28, rate the levels of emotion you experienced while practicing the behavior (0 = complete lack of the emotion; 10 = a high level of the emotion).
4. After you've completed a few practice sessions, your difficulty levels and your depression/sadness and anxiety/irritability levels should decrease, while your pleasure/satisfaction levels should gradually increase. The idea is to continue working on the same target behavior until you notice substantial changes in your levels. It's okay if this takes longer than one week. Just keep working at it until you notice substantial changes. Some very challenging behaviors may take several weeks to become more comfortable. When one step becomes less challenging, you'll be ready to move on to the next step toward your goal.

DATE PRACTICED	ANTICIPATED DIFFICULTY (0–10)	ACTUAL DIFFICULTY (0–10)	DEPRESSION/ SADNESS (0–10)	ANXIETY/ IRRITABILITY (0–10)	PLEASURE/ SATISFACTION (0–10)	OTHER (0–10)

STEP ELEVEN

Once you've reached your goal, assess what went well and what didn't. Use that information to help decide which behavior to target next.

Next Target Behavior:

YOUR WORK LIFE ACTION PLAN

Now let's take all the information you've gathered on your target behaviors, potential obstacles, and rewards and create an action plan for your first work life goal.

Target Behavior:

Specific Goal:

Problems/Obstacles:

Solutions/Modifications:

Potential Avoidance Behaviors:

Alternatives to Avoidance Behaviors:

Behavior Reinforcement:

Steps to Take:

1.

2.

3.

4.

5.

Anticipated Rewards for Success:

DATE PRACTICED	ANTICIPATED DIFFICULTY (0–10)	ACTUAL DIFFICULTY (0–10)	DEPRESSION/ SADNESS (0–10)	ANXIETY/ IRRITABILITY (0–10)	PLEASURE/ SATISFACTION (0–10)	OTHER (0–10)

Next Target Behavior:

REVIEWING YOUR PROGRESS

Now that you've set an initial goal for your work life and practiced your target behavior, let's assess your progress. Respond to the following prompts in the spaces provided:

How did you feel when you completed this goal?

Were there any unexpected challenges? If so, what were they?

Was anything easier than expected?

How did you overcome the obstacles you encountered?

Should you try to take on a less challenging task next time, or are you ready to increase the intensity?

_____

_____

_____

How difficult will it be to maintain your new behavior?

_____

_____

_____

How can you overcome obstacles that could interfere with engaging in this behavior in the future?

_____

_____

_____

TAKEAWAYS

- Symptoms of trauma can make it difficult to function in your professional life.
- Triggers are reminders of things that have happened to us in the past, and we respond to them with the same emotions we felt toward the original experience.
- Concentration practice can help keep your attention in the moment and help you regain the ability to focus.
- Passive, aggressive, passive-aggressive, and assertive styles of communication are the different ways we deal with conflict. Assertive communication is the healthiest style.
- Coping with vocational stress can lead to a variety of avoidance behaviors that interfere with your ability to do your job and can even impact other areas of your life.

SOCIAL AND RECREATIONAL LIFE

THE BASICS

How people choose to socialize or spend their free time differs dramatically from one person to another. Maybe you have a few close friends you like to see every once in a while, or you have a contact list that is hundreds strong and you never spend an evening alone. You may play in multiple sport leagues throughout the year or alternatively have only one or two hobbies that you focus on in your spare time. It doesn't matter if you think of yourself as an introvert, an extrovert, or somewhere in between. As you think about your PTSD symptoms and how they interfere with this area of your life, it's important to compare and contrast your current social and recreational life with your actual social and recreational needs, and not with what others think is normal and healthy.

What types of changes have you noticed in the way you socialize or spend your downtime since your traumatic experience? If your trauma happened many years ago, perhaps during your childhood, how do you think it shaped your social and recreational choices as an adult? Chances are, whenever your trauma occurred, it has impacted you a lot more than you think. While you may recognize some of the biggest differences and challenges, it may be that you haven't even uncovered some of the subtler ways trauma has infiltrated your social and recreational life.

It's time to thoroughly review this part of your life to make sure your actions match your values—does your social life look the way you want it to? Or is your PTSD making you avoidant, causing you to miss out on people and events you care about?

In this section, you'll look at the ways PTSD has impacted relationships with your friends, family, and acquaintances; the hobbies and activities you choose to participate in; the way you feel about your own behavior; and the way you respond in a variety of social and recreational situations. You'll then identify your goals, figure out how to reach them, and work on developing alternatives to your avoidance behaviors.

HOW IS YOUR SOCIAL AND RECREATIONAL LIFE?

Earlier, we introduced you to John (see page 44). John's trauma-related symptoms impact his social life in subtle ways. He likes spending time with people he knows well; he's uncomfortable around new people, and it takes him time to think of someone as a friend. He prefers small, quiet social events with his family over activities in crowded places with lots of unfamiliar people. Most of the time this works well, but his kids are getting older and have started asking to go to the types of places that make him uneasy, like amusement parks and malls—the crowded places he tried to avoid. This is starting to cause conflict within his family.

In the last year, John has joined an archery club and really loves competing with himself to better his scores. He's also made some new friends and feels comfortable laughing and talking with them at the club, but when they make plans to meet somewhere else, he often says yes but cancels later. A week ago, he was scheduled to be part of a big multi-club tournament, but he cancelled at the last minute even though he knew that his teammates were depending on him. He was too worried that he'd be overwhelmed with anxiety at the large, crowded venue. Now, he feels terrible about disappointing them and worries that they must think he's a flake.

There are many ways PTSD can interfere with your social and recreational life choices. You may relate to some of John's struggles, or you may have a completely different set of symptoms and avoidance behaviors to contend with. Like we've done in prior sections, let's look at some of the ways PTSD symptoms can interfere with your social and recreational life.

Fear is a normal reaction to a dangerous or threatening situation, but extreme and/ or chronic threats can affect this helpful response. Once damaged, the fear response triggers "false alarms" that can lead to hyperarousal or the feeling of being chronically on guard. Obviously, this is extremely unpleasant and often leads to anxiety when you engage in activities that make you uncomfortable. Over time, the size of your comfort zone decreases until you only feel comfortable doing a few activities.

Intrusive thoughts can be triggered by a wide variety of people, places, and things. Sometimes you may anticipate events that will trigger these painful memories, but other times you may be taken by surprise. It can be embarrassing to have strong emotional responses that others around you may not understand, particularly if you're away from home. This can make you wary about trying new activities or going out with people you don't know very well. It can even make you hesitant to go out with your closest friends.

Because socializing and recreation frequently take us outside our comfort zone, the activities that should be enjoyable are often disrupted by these physiological experiences. Once you've experienced acute anxiety, you may start to anticipate situations that could trigger episodes and get the urge to avoid them altogether.

Anger can also pose a significant obstacle in your social and recreational life. Whether you keep your frustration bottled up or express it openly, anger and irritability can impact your ability to enjoy yourself and connect with people. If you're frequently irritated with yourself or with others, you may decide to give up the things you used to enjoy or you may drop activities because you worry about acting out on your feelings. And if displays of verbal or physical aggression have become a problem for you, it may be that others don't want to socialize with you.

UNCOVERING TARGET BEHAVIORS

To identify specific goals, let's look at how you're performing on some tasks that are often part of a good-quality social and recreational life. Some of the activities listed here may not be relevant to you; that's okay. You may also identify more than one area where you are experiencing a great deal of challenge or not meeting your basic responsibilities. If this is the case, you can prioritize the tasks that are currently having the most impact on your quality of life when you move on to identifying target behaviors.

Rate the following skills/activities according to this scale:
0 = N/A, 1 = Never, 2 = Almost never, 3 = Rarely, 4 = On occasion,
5 = Sometimes, 6 = Less frequently, 7 = Frequently, 8 = More frequently,
9 = Most of the time, 10 = Always

SOCIAL AND RECREATIONAL LIFE SKILLS/ACTIVITIES	MY RATINGS
SELF-CARE	
I have hobbies or things I enjoy doing just for fun.	
Learning something new is enjoyable.	
I have hobbies or skills that I'm good at.	
I have some type of physical activity that I enjoy (e.g., exercising, martial arts, sports).	
I pick books or movies that I enjoy.	
I have a hobby that helps me relax or unwind when alone.	
I participate in enjoyable clubs, organizations, or religious groups.	
Find your average score by dividing the total by the number of answers with a score higher than 0.	

(CONTINUED)

SOCIAL AND RECREATIONAL LIFE SKILLS/ACTIVITIES (CONTINUED)	MY RATINGS
SAFETY AND SECURITY	
I feel safe and secure in social settings without exercising excessive caution.	
I can take any available seat no matter where it's placed or what it's facing.	
I can go to crowded places or places where people congregate (e.g., movies, shopping malls, restaurants).	
I can use public transportation (bus, train, airplane) when needed.	
I can be a passenger in a car.	
I can tolerate loud cheering at sporting events or concerts.	
I can tolerate the noise and unexpected movements of animals and small children when I'm visiting others.	
Find your average score by dividing the total by the number of answers with a score higher than 0.	
INTERACTING WITH OTHERS	
I'm able to tolerate oblivious or inconsiderate behavior of others (e.g., carts blocking aisles in stores, people talking loudly on cell phones, etc.).	
I'm comfortable with the number of friends and social contacts I have.	
I can make and keep plans with other people.	
I can engage in small talk.	
I communicate with others in a reasonable way about things that are triggering for me.	
I feel comfortable inviting someone for an outing or date.	
I feel comfortable inviting people to my home.	
I include people I care about in my recreational or social activities.	

INTERACTING WITH OTHERS (CONTINUED)	MY RATINGS
I can address conflicts with friends in a reasonable manner.	
I don't avoid conflicts with friends.	
Find your average score by dividing the total by the number of answers with a score higher than 0.	

GENERAL TASKS/RESPONSIBILITIES	
I can stand in line and wait.	
I'm able to participate in and enjoy group activities.	
I make plans to do things in the future that I think I might enjoy (e.g., concerts, plays, sporting matches).	
I can participate in recreation while sober.	
I'm able to maintain focus and concentration on a project.	
I can cope with stressful or unexpected situations.	
I enjoy reading/watching TV/playing video games in moderation and can focus enough to follow along with the story.	
I can read and follow directions for a hobby (e.g., putting something together like a model, following recipes).	
I can tolerate traffic.	
Find your average score by dividing the total by the number of answers that have a score higher than 0.	

Look at your average score for each section:

- If you scored 1 to 3 in any section, make this area a priority when choosing your target behaviors.
- If you scored 4 to 7 in any section, target these behaviors once you've addressed any higher priority areas of concern.
- If you scored 8 to 10 in any section, you're functioning well in that area.

WHAT ARE YOUR TRIGGERS?

In prior sections, we discussed the ways you may be triggered at home or work. Now let's dive into triggers that might arise in social or recreational settings. If you're reading the life domains out of order and haven't read section 3 yet, turn to page 49 and read about triggers. It's essential to understand what they are so you can identify your own triggers in the following exercise.

> Two summers ago, Cho and a friend were visiting a city in a non-English-speaking country. It was a beautiful, warm evening, and they were walking slowly along a wide sidewalk, stopping at each restaurant they passed to inquire about available outside seating. A car sped past them and sideswiped another car before spinning out of control into a group of people right in front of them.

> Despite the fact that they couldn't understand the instructions being yelled by those around them, Cho and his friend helped the injured. Unfortunately, they weren't able to save everyone, and Cho held the hand of a young man as he died. Since that night, Cho is unwilling to eat out. He has significant trouble walking in big cities and can feel his heart rate spike when he hears people yelling or talking loudly in languages he can't understand. Cho has always jogged to stay fit, but lately he's had to stop because as his heart rate climbs, his memory is flooded with the images of all of the broken people he saw that night and the screams of their panicked loved ones.

As you've already learned, memories, physical sensations, and emotions are all *internal triggers*. Just like Cho's reaction to jogging, it may be that the reason you're anxious, feeling lonely, or have a racing heart has nothing to do with your traumatic experience, but your brain has linked those feelings to the feelings you experienced as a result of your traumatic event. This is what causes your PTSD symptoms to engage. For Cho, conflicts with others who don't follow his idea of safe driving habits can also activate his symptoms. For example, he gets extremely angry when he sees someone speeding or driving erratically. He's even gotten into arguments and ended relationships with friends who drank a single beer or glass of wine before driving.

Again, *external triggers* are things like sights, sounds, or smells. For Cho, these are things like hearing the sound of sirens or people talking loudly in a foreign language, smelling food like that served in the nearby restaurant, or hearing anything that sounds like the car as it jumped the sidewalk and crashed. When he encounters one of these triggers, he knows his PTSD symptoms are about to engage.

An effective way to reduce your symptoms is to prepare for your triggers. Knowing what they are and when they will activate lets you choose the way you'll respond when they do kick in. Over time, your symptoms will decrease and you'll be able to get back to your regular activities and living a satisfying life.

For each of the following symptom categories, list anything you've noticed that triggers those symptoms in your social or recreational life. Keep in mind that one trigger can initiate multiple symptoms, so you may list the same trigger in more than one category. You may even want to ask trusted friends or loved ones to help you pinpoint any triggers they've observed.

Anxiety

Anger

Panic Attacks/Physiological Responses

Depression

_____

_____

_____

Flashbacks and Intrusive Thoughts

_____

_____

_____

Nightmares

_____

_____

_____

Being aware of your triggers can help you put a plan in place to head them off before your symptoms become unmanageable.

Talking About Your Trauma

Talking about trauma is difficult. In fact, it's so tough that not wanting to speak or even think about it is one of the symptoms of PTSD. Maybe you want to discuss what happened and what you're experiencing now, but you worry about how others will respond or you don't want to burden your loved ones with what you see as your load to carry.

Maybe you worry that admitting your trauma is still impacting you months or even years after it happened makes you seem weak or unable to cope as well as others who have experienced the same types of events. While internal strength has nothing to do with whether a trauma survivor will go on to develop PTSD, worrying about appearing weak can discourage you from speaking to others about it. In addition, you may fear that others might judge you harshly for the things you did or didn't do during or after the traumatic event. These are all normal concerns for trauma survivors who are thinking about sharing their stories with someone who hasn't heard them before.

However, one of the things that can help you heal is to repeatedly talk about your trauma. Think about it this way: If you're afraid to talk about what happened, it has power over you. Every time you talk about it, the horror of your experience stings a little less. Maybe you need to talk about it so a friend will understand your symptoms or you want to help prepare them for an upcoming situation that could be triggering. Sometimes you simply need the support of a loved one who knows what happened to you.

It's always up to you how much to say. You don't have to share every detail if it makes you uncomfortable, but it's important to remember that the quality of support you get from others will be influenced by what you tell them. Giving instruction or feedback about how you would like to receive support or why you react the way you do will really help those around you understand how to offer their support. With that said, it's important to remember that the people you tell are not responsible for your emotional reactions and it's not their job to make sure that you don't get triggered. Have a plan in place for how you'll react if a conversation about your trauma triggers your symptoms.

Well-meaning family, friends, and coworkers want to offer support, but they don't always know the best way to approach you or bring up the topic of your trauma. Often they say nothing at all, and your trauma becomes the elephant in the room. Or, if they do talk to you about your trauma, they may be insensitive or give unhelpful suggestions. Obviously, this can be frustrating or even hurtful, but it's important to keep in mind that most people aren't purposefully trying to upset you. They might be afraid to ask questions or bring up the topic because they don't want to say the wrong thing or they're afraid to remind you of the traumatic experience. They may also worry about their own emotional reactions. Having a conversation about their worries can help reassure them that you know their intentions are good and that you'll tell them if they say something inappropriate or if they ask a question you don't want to answer.

Not everyone will be a good source of emotional support. If you're not sure how someone will react, do a test run. Share one piece of your experience and then decide what else, if anything, you're going to say. Some people might surprise you with their responses, both in good and bad ways. Don't be shocked if you get support from a completely unexpected source. Any support is good support. Take what others offer; it will help as you move through the recovery process.

When you first tell someone about your trauma or PTSD, the conversation can be a little awkward. It might be easiest to start with how your experience is impacting you right now and how they can help you.

The following are some examples of information you can give to people who already know something about your trauma:

- "Today is the anniversary of my trauma, and I want some time alone."

- "I feel uncomfortable sitting with my back to the door."

- "Sirens remind me of the event."

If you want to initiate a conversation to tell someone you've experienced a traumatic event, you can say something along the lines of:

- "I want to tell you something important, but it's difficult for me to talk about, and it might be difficult for you to hear. Last year *(e.g., I was in a terrible accident, my child died, I was assaulted, I was shot, etc.).* Since then, I've been having symptoms of PTSD."

- "I would like to tell you why I *(e.g., jump at loud noises, can't sit with my back to the door, don't like to go to the movie theater, etc.).* I have PTSD from a traumatic experience, and this is one of my symptoms."

If you need someone to have a basic understanding of your experience, but don't want to explain anything, here are a few examples:

- "I had a traumatic experience, and this is one of my symptoms. I know you may have questions, but I'm not ready to talk about it."

- "Something terrible happened to me last year, and this is one of my symptoms. I don't need you to do anything about it, but I want you to know that this is the reason I *(e.g., don't like to fly, would rather not attend the surprise party, reacted so strongly to the fire alarm, etc.).*"

If you have a loved one who is supportive and helpful but seems reluctant to ask questions or bring up the topic, try this:

- "I appreciate your support. I want you to feel like you can talk to me or ask me questions about my trauma/PTSD. If I don't want to talk about it or answer your questions, I'll let you know."

WHAT ARE YOUR AVOIDANCE BEHAVIORS?

Kobe has always loved music, so when his favorite band reunited for a farewell tour he was determined to go to the concert. He chose seats near the exit and asked his brother to go with him. As he usually does before social events, he had a few drinks before the show to prepare for what he knew would be a challenging situation. When the lights went down and the music started, Kobe was overcome by apprehension. He made it through the first song and a half before telling his brother he was going to the restroom. Kobe spent the rest of the show waiting for his brother in the parking lot.

Avoidance makes it hard to stay active and social. Movies, restaurants, concerts, malls, and amusement parks are fun for a lot of people, but they are challenging when they trigger anxiety. Even when you're looking forward to an activity or event, strong urges to escape, avoid, or engage in safety behaviors can emerge. Avoidance is not always obvious and easy to recognize, like it was when Kobe left the concert early. Avoidance is also the need to choose a safe seat, using alcohol or drugs before participating in a stressful activity, or anything else that prevents you from fully engaging in the experience. You may cancel plans at the last minute, avoid going to other people's homes, refuse to ride as a passenger in a car, or be very choosy about the location of your seat in a public venue.

EXERCISE   YOUR AVOIDANCE BEHAVIORS

Contemplate the avoidance behaviors you use in your social or recreational life. In this worksheet, list your avoidance behaviors in the first column. In the second column, identify the situations in which you use those behaviors to cope.

AVOIDANCE BEHAVIOR	I USE THIS BEHAVIOR WHEN . . .

HOW IS AVOIDANCE WORKING FOR YOU?

Even though avoidance behaviors cause problems in your social or recreational life, they wouldn't have developed into habits if they didn't offer you some relief from your symptoms. Think about the avoidance behaviors you identified in the previous exercise that help you cope in social and recreational settings. For example, maybe you deal with your anxiety by leaving a place that makes you uncomfortable, like a restaurant. While you may feel immediate relief from your symptoms, the inconvenience your behaviors cause for the friends and family who you socialize and recreate with can damage your relationships.

EXERCISE   YOUR AVOIDANCE GAINS AND LOSSES

It's important to recognize the positives and negatives associated with the social and recreational life avoidance strategies you've been relying on. That way, you can anticipate potential challenges as you start changing your behavior. Respond to the following prompts in the spaces provided.

Describe a social or recreational situation that triggers an avoidance behavior and explain exactly how you react.

What are the payoffs for avoiding this situation?

_____

_____

_____

_____

What are the negatives of avoiding this situation?

_____

_____

_____

_____

WHAT ARE YOUR ALTERNATIVES?

Avoidance behaviors help relieve the discomfort of anxiety. However, now that you understand the consequences of avoidance behavior, it's time to think about alternatives that are more in line with your values and goals. Take it slowly. It's okay if your current behavior is far from where you'd like it to be. As you master this process, taking one small step at a time, you'll be able to take on greater challenges in the weeks and months to come.

Pay attention to successful coping strategies already in place and apply them in areas where you're still struggling. For example, if concentrating on regulating your breathing is an effective way to offset feelings of panic when you're introduced to people you don't know, try the same approach when you're shown to a table in the middle of a crowded restaurant.

If you're reading the life sections out of order, go back to page 58 in section 3 for more detailed information on this topic before moving on to the following exercise.

EXERCISE   YOUR ALTERNATIVES

Review the avoidance behaviors you identified in the exercise "Your Avoidance Behaviors" on page 109 that have negative consequences in your social and recreational life. It's time to consider your alternatives. Respond to the following prompts in the spaces provided.

Think about the negative consequences or costs of your avoidance behaviors. How do they interfere with your long-term goals?

(For example: I don't like to sit in the middle of a room or where I can't see the exit. This makes it difficult to go see a movie or out to dinner with my friends. When I go out, I make people change places with me so I get the seat that I want. Sometimes I even make them switch restaurants if there are no good seats. This annoys my friends. Sometimes they go out without me because it's easier than putting up with my demands. I really value my friendships, and my behavior is interfering with them.)

What could you try instead? List three to five options for alternative responses.

(For example: I can agree to refrain from asking my friends to switch seats or change restaurants. When I'm seated in a place that makes me uncomfortable, I can remind myself that I'm safe and that my anxiety doesn't mean that I'm in danger. I could also practice sitting in an uncomfortable position in a less crowded restaurant.)

BREAKING DOWN TARGET BEHAVIORS

Refer back to the challenge areas you identified in the exercise "Uncovering Target Behaviors" on page 101. Choose a behavior to target. Every time you practice your target behavior, you will be building a new habit.

In this exercise, you'll identify some smaller goals or steps you can take to increase your chance of success. Some of these steps may be uncomfortable and require multiple repetitions before you're ready to move on to the next step. Fill in all of your anticipated difficulty ratings now, before you even begin to practice them. It's okay if some of your numbers are very high—they will decrease as you practice.

If one of your steps involves doing the activity with someone you know, it's a good idea to explain what you're doing before you start. This will help them understand your behavior if you get uncomfortable and make it easier for you to stay on track.

Here is an example to get you started:

Target Behavior: Go to crowded places or places where people congregate (movies, shopping malls, restaurants).

Specific Goal: Attend a sporting event where there will be loud cheering.

STEPS I CAN TAKE RIGHT NOW TO REACH MY GOAL	ANTICIPATED DIFFICULTY 0 = easy, 5 = moderately uncomfortable, 10 = impossible
Watch a professional sporting event alone at home where I will be able to hear loud cheering on the broadcast.	4
From a distance, watch a local sporting event like a school or recreational children's league with small, but enthusiastic crowds.	5
From the spectators' area, attend a local sporting event like a school or recreational children's league with small, but enthusiastic crowds.	7
Stand just outside the gates of a local sporting event like a high school football or basketball game with an enthusiastic crowd.	6
Invite a few friends over to watch a professional sporting event in my home.	7
Go to a restaurant or bar to watch a professional sporting event on television with cheering fans around me.	8
Attend a local sporting event like a high school football or basketball game with a large crowd.	9
Attend a professional sporting event with a trusted companion who is aware of my triggers and willing to help keep me focused on my goal.	9

Target Behavior:

Specific Goal:

STEPS I CAN TAKE RIGHT NOW TO REACH MY GOAL	ANTICIPATED DIFFICULTY 0 = easy, 5 = moderately uncomfortable, 10 = impossible

Now that you have an idea of what steps you can take toward your target behavior, identify any obstacles you might encounter and how you will overcome them so that you have a plan in place.

What obstacles might prevent you from practicing?

(For example: It might rain on the day I planned to attend an outdoor sporting event.)

_____

_____

How can you overcome these obstacles?

(For example: I will choose seats under the overhang or look for alternative dates that I could attend.)

_____

_____

ACTION PLAN FOR CHANGE

It's time to create an action plan to help you strategize and make key decisions before a triggering social or recreational situation arises. Some new behaviors will be immediately rewarding, such as getting back into a favorite hobby, but others might take a little time to display their benefits. To identify appropriate goals, consider your values (you will do this in the first step).

Values are important because they remind us of the direction we want to head in. After determining the direction you want to travel, focus on identifying a moderately challenging goal and the type of reinforcement you'll need to stay motivated. Consider creating a reward system for practicing. This should be something you look forward to like playing a video game for a set period of time or going for a hike on your day off. Figure out what will motivate you to keep moving forward, even when things become challenging.

STEP ONE

In section 2, you identified your top three values (see page 27). Reflect on these values and consider how they apply to your social and recreational life. Ultimately, multiple values will come into play, but for now start with one you think is most important for this area and write it in the space provided.

Value:

STEP TWO

Think of a target behavior that relates to that value and identify your specific goal. Write them in the spaces provided. (Remember, if your target behavior doesn't have a set number of repetitions, try to practice a minimum of four times during the next week.)

Target Behavior:

Specific Goal:

STEP THREE

What problems or obstacles do you think you might encounter as you work toward your goal?

Problems/Obstacles:
....

STEP FOUR

What solutions or modifications can you try if problems or obstacles arise?

Solutions/Modifications:
....

STEP FIVE

What avoidance behaviors do you think you might want to participate in as you challenge yourself?

Potential Avoidance Behaviors:
....

STEP SIX

What can you try instead of the avoidance behaviors?

Alternatives to Avoidance Behaviors:
....

STEP SEVEN

What will reinforce your new behavior?

Behavior Reinforcement:
....

STEP EIGHT

Review the exercise "Breaking Down Target Behaviors" on page 114. In the space provided, write down the steps you can take to work up to your ultimate goal. These steps will help you identify new behaviors to target as you achieve mastery of your initial target behaviors.

Steps to Take:

1. ....

2. ....

3. ....

4. ....

5. ....

STEP NINE

When you reach your goal or complete your target behavior, what type of reward do you expect to receive? This may be a personal sense of accomplishment or satisfaction, or some external reward like the appreciation of a friend.

Rewards for Success: ....

STEP TEN

In the worksheet, record the results from your practice sessions. If necessary, review the exercise "Evaluating Your Progress" on page 40.

1. Record the date of each practice session.
2. Using the scale from the exercise "Degree of Difficulty," fill in your anticipated difficulty levels and actual difficulty levels (0 = completely relaxed and at peace; 10 = most distressed, unable to think clearly, fight/flight/freeze response engage).
3. Using the scale from the exercise "What Are You Doing Now?" on page 28, rate the levels of emotion you experienced while practicing the behavior (0 = complete lack of the emotion; 10 = a high level of the emotion).
4. After you've completed a few practice sessions, your difficulty levels and your depression/sadness and anxiety/irritability levels should decrease, while your pleasure/satisfaction levels should gradually increase. The idea is to continue working on the same target behavior until you notice substantial changes in your levels. It's okay if this takes longer than one week. Some very challenging behaviors may take several weeks to become more comfortable. Just keep working at it until you notice substantial changes. When one step becomes less challenging, you'll be ready to move on to the next step toward your goal.

DATE PRACTICED	ANTICIPATED DIFFICULTY (0–10)	ACTUAL DIFFICULTY (0–10)	DEPRESSION/ SADNESS (0–10)	ANXIETY/ IRRITABILITY (0–10)	PLEASURE/ SATISFACTION (0–10)	OTHER (0–10)

STEP ELEVEN

Once you've reached your goal, assess what went well and what didn't. Use that information to help decide which behavior to target next.

Next Target Behavior:

YOUR SOCIAL AND RECREATIONAL LIFE ACTION PLAN

Now let's take all the information you've gathered on your target behaviors, potential obstacles, and rewards and create an action plan for your first social and recreational life goal.

Target Behavior:

Specific Goal:

Problems/Obstacles:

Solutions/Modifications:

Potential Avoidance Behaviors:

Alternatives to Avoidance Behaviors:

Behavior Reinforcement:

Steps to Take:

1.

2.

3.

4.

5.

Anticipated Rewards for Success:

DATE PRACTICED	ANTICIPATED DIFFICULTY (0–10)	ACTUAL DIFFICULTY (0–10)	DEPRESSION/ SADNESS (0–10)	ANXIETY/ IRRITABILITY (0–10)	PLEASURE/ SATISFACTION (0–10)	OTHER (0–10)

Next Target Behavior:

REVIEWING YOUR PROGRESS

Now that you've set an initial goal for your social and recreational life and practiced your target behavior, let's assess your progress. Respond to the following prompts in the spaces provided:

How did you feel when you completed this goal?

_____

_____

_____

Were there any unexpected challenges? If so, what were they?

_____

_____

_____

Was anything easier than expected?

_____

_____

_____

How did you overcome the obstacles you encountered?

_____

_____

_____

Should you try to take on a less challenging task next time, or are you ready to increase the intensity?

_____

_____

_____

How difficult will it be to maintain your new behavior?

_____

_____

_____

How can you overcome obstacles that could interfere with engaging in this behavior in the future?

_____

_____

_____

TAKEAWAYS

- It can be difficult to have a satisfying social and recreational life when you are experiencing significant PTSD symptoms.
- Identifying social and recreational goals in keeping with your values can help you to return to healthy activities that you have been avoiding.
- Triggers are reminders of things that have happened to us in the past, and we respond to them with the same emotions we felt toward the original experience.
- You can share your traumatic experiences and PTSD struggles with others so they understand what's happening when you're triggered.
- It's important to tackle your avoidance behaviors so you can achieve your goals of enjoying social and recreational activities.

HEALTH AND WELLNESS

THE BASICS

WITHOUT A DOUBT, focusing on your physical, mental, and spiritual health and wellness is one of the most important things you can do for yourself. As you already know, symptoms of PTSD can disrupt your ability to care for yourself properly in all aspects of your life. However, unlike in the other life domains, there are some well-researched health and wellness standards that you—and everyone else—should try to meet. These include things like exercising regularly; eating a well-balanced diet; refraining from tobacco use or overindulging in alcohol, drugs, or food; and seeing a doctor and dentist regularly.

In addition, you should attempt to meet your own personal standards of grooming and, if you're so inclined, attend to your spiritual needs. Finally, as you're doing right now by reading this book, you should pay attention to your psychological health, especially when you're struggling with something like PTSD, which has the ability to derail your entire life and everything you value.

As you think about your PTSD symptoms and how they interfere with the life domain of health and wellness, it's important to look at where you are right now and set reasonable goals in conjunction with where you and your doctor, therapist, and/or religious or spiritual guide think you should be. If you're a couch potato, we're not looking to turn you into a marathon runner. We just want to help you find the best level of health for you.

How has your approach to your mental, physical, and spiritual health changed since your traumatic experience? If your trauma happened during childhood or if many years have passed since the event, in what ways do you think it's shaped the health and wellness choices you make today? Whenever your trauma occurred, there's a good chance it's impacted you a lot more than you realize in terms of your health and wellness. Chances are you may recognize some of the biggest differences and challenges, but there's likely even more to uncover.

In this section, you'll thoroughly review your health and wellness to verify that the actions you take in the self-care department match your values. You'll look at the ways PTSD has influenced your health and wellness choices and the way you feel about your own behavior, determining how the choices you make in different situations affect your overall health and wellness. You'll then identify your goals, figure out how to reach them, and work on developing alternatives to your avoidance behaviors.

HOW ARE YOU TAKING CARE OF YOURSELF?

Let's revisit John (see page 44). John played team sports when he was young and has been physically fit for most of his life. However, he's gained 20 pounds and knows it's because he's not eating well, and his weekly visit to his archery club is his only physical activity. John doesn't do drugs and although he does drink alcohol socially, he's careful not to overindulge. But when John is stressed, he chooses unhealthy foods and often doesn't stop eating when he's full. He thinks about going to the gym and knows it would help him feel better, but it seems like there's always something more important for him to do.

John suspects his blood pressure is higher than it should be, but he's avoided checking in with his doctor for the past couple of years. He's embarrassed about his weight gain and always tells himself that this is the week he's going to start eating better and exercising, and then he'll call to schedule a checkup.

Before John was sexually abused, he attended church with his mom. For a period of time after the assault, they both preferred to stay at home, avoiding the questions from the other parishioners and the accusations from their own extended family. Eventually, his mom returned to the church, but John refused to join her. Now John's wife takes their children to church every Sunday, but John only attends on special occasions, such as holidays or if his wife begs him to go. He has not lost his faith and he would like to attend regularly, but he worries constantly about being judged by others, and it's less stressful to stay at home.

Maybe you recognize some of John's symptoms in your own life. Obviously, you've noticed changes in your mental health since developing PTSD, but have you also noticed changes in your physical or spiritual health?

There are many ways PTSD can impact your health and wellness. Not only are your symptoms distracting and frustrating, they can damage your physical health. The prolonged physiological arousal of the fight, flight, or freeze response and symptoms that often co-occur with PTSD, such as general anxiety, depressed mood, and anger, are all associated with health-related problems.

According to research, trauma survivors have a higher incidence of several types of medical conditions than people without a history of trauma. Some of these areas include cardiovascular disease (e.g., hypertension, stroke, and heart attack), respiratory disease (e.g., asthma), autoimmune conditions (e.g., rheumatoid arthritis, thyroid conditions, multiple sclerosis, and lupus), musculoskeletal disorders (e.g., arthritis and fibromyalgia), metabolic disorders (e.g., diabetes, high cholesterol), chronic pain, cancer, susceptibility to infections, and gastrointestinal conditions (e.g., irritable bowel syndrome and ulcers). Even if you haven't been diagnosed with a specific condition, your physical health symptoms, such as headaches, digestive upset, and pain, may increase during times of stress.

It's hard to take care of yourself when you're in a constant state of anxiety and can't relax or engage in the activities that help you feel physically and mentally restored. When you can't unwind, you may feel chronically exhausted and that you don't have the energy to be at your best in other areas of your life.

Repeated unwanted thoughts interfere with a range of healthy activities, and it's not uncommon to cope with such unpleasant images and feelings with unhealthy self-soothing. Avoidance behaviors commonly used to self-soothe include drinking, drug use, smoking, gambling, overspending, excessive eating, risky sexual behaviors, and compulsive use of pornography. All can be detrimental to your physical, mental, and/or spiritual health.

Depression can strip us of the motivation to do the things that make us feel good. Fatigue caused by depression can make it hard to do even the basic things you need to do to care for yourself and your family. Engaging in the behaviors that you consider physically and emotionally healthy may seem like too much work. Moreover, individuals who experienced abuse or neglect as a child can also struggle with healthy habits since they lacked positive role models and nurturing caregivers.

The tension of long-term anger is damaging to your emotional and physical health. Not to mention that anger and irritability often keep you from engaging in activities with others that might improve your physical and emotional well-being.

UNCOVERING TARGET BEHAVIORS

To identify specific goals, let's look at how you're performing the tasks that fall under the health and wellness category. Some of the activities listed may not be relevant to you; that's okay. You may also identify more than one area where you are experiencing a great deal of challenge or not meeting your basic responsibilities. If this is the case, you can prioritize the tasks that are currently having the most impact on your quality of life when you move on to identifying target behaviors.

Rate the following skills/activities according to this scale:
0 = N/A, 1 = Never, 2 = Almost never, 3 = Rarely, 4 = On occasion,
5 = Sometimes, 6 = Less frequently, 7 = Frequently, 8 = More frequently,
9 = Most of the time, 10 = Always

HEALTH AND WELLNESS SKILLS/ACTIVITIES	MY RATINGS
SELF-CARE	
I eat a healthy, balanced diet.	
I exercise regularly.	
I follow medical advice/take medication as prescribed.	
I follow a regular sleep schedule.	
I'm able to get a full night's sleep.	
I don't abuse drugs or alcohol.	
I don't use tobacco products.	
I regulate my use of caffeine.	
I address mental health issues and follow appropriate treatment.	
I have a healthy sex life.	
Find your average score by dividing the total by the number of answers with a score higher than 0.	

	MY RATINGS
SAFETY AND SECURITY	
I don't engage in self-injurious behavior.	
I don't contemplate suicide.	
I avoid dangerous or reckless behavior.	
I don't drink/get high and drive.	
Find your average score by dividing the total by the number of answers with a score higher than 0.	
GENERAL TASKS/RESPONSIBILITIES	
I go to the doctor/dentist for regular checkups.	
I make appointments in a timely manner and keep them.	
I avoid using unhealthy habits to cope with my feelings (e.g., excessive gambling, compulsive pornography, impulsive unsafe sex, impulsive spending, compulsive eating, excessive video gaming).	
I can adjust habits in order to treat chronic health issues.	
I avoid activities that are known to worsen chronic health issues.	
I treat physical pain.	
Find your average score by dividing the total by the number of answers that have a score higher than 0.	

Look at your average score for each section:

- If you scored 1 to 3 in any section, make this area a priority when choosing your target behaviors.
- If you scored 4 to 7 in any section, target these behaviors once you've addressed any higher priority areas of concern.
- If you scored 8 to 10 in any section, you're functioning well in that area.

WHAT ARE YOUR TRIGGERS?

By now, you probably have a pretty good idea of your main triggers. If you're reading the life domains out of order and have not read section 3 yet, turn to page 49 and read about triggers. It's important that you understand them so you can identify your own triggers in the following exercise.

Sean was a New York City firefighter on 9/11. His childhood best friend, Derek, was in his same unit, and they were on duty together as the initial calls came in. They worked side by side for more than 36 hours straight and for endless days that followed as they searched the rubble for survivors and then for remains. Eventually, Sean and Derek resumed some version of a normal life, but neither one could forget the horror of their experience and the loss of so many good friends and neighbors. Sean eventually left the fire department and got a job in an office near his home.

For years, the friends met weekly to have a few drinks and yell at their favorite teams on the big screen at the corner bar. Once or twice a year, and only if they were very drunk, they talked about what they'd seen and done in the days after the towers fell. During their last conversation about their mutual trauma, Derek told Sean that he wished he'd died in the attack so he didn't have to live with the images that were stuck on repeat in his head. That night, Derek committed suicide.

Months have passed, and Sean feels responsible for Derek's death. He knows how relentless the memories are, how his heart stops every time he sees an airplane flying a little too close to the city, and how difficult it is to get up the energy to go to work each day. He knew that his friend was struggling and feels like he should have done more to help.

After a particularly bad day at work, Sean enters his apartment and is overwhelmed by the screech of the smoke detector and the acrid smell of something burning on the stove. His wife is up on a chair, trying to push open the tiny window above the sink to release the visible haze of smoky air. Sean's heart rate skyrockets, and he feels compelled to handle a situation that his wife already has under control. He roughly picks her up and sets her off to one side, kicks the chair the other direction, pushes open the window, and yells about how she knows he can't stand the smell of something burning. He stomps out of the apartment and goes to the corner bar he used to visit with Derek. He can't believe he treated his wife like that. He feels like he's letting everyone down. The memories of 9/11 won't stop tormenting him, and he can't stop thinking about Derek's suicide. He feels like things will never get better and that maybe Derek was right to check out when he did.

Just like Sean's reaction to fearing for his wife, or his thoughts and emotions about Derek's suicide, if you're sad, feeling claustrophobic, are easily startled, or feeling nervous for a reason that has nothing to do with your traumatic experience, but your brain has linked those feelings to the feelings to trauma, then your PTSD symptoms will activate. These *internal triggers* can be emotions, physical sensations, or memories.

Sean's *external triggers* are things like the smell or sight of smoke, seeing or hearing a plane near the city, the sound of the fire bell ringing as he walks past a station, and hearing a large number of sirens. Even a very foggy day with low visibility can trigger his symptoms because it reminds him of the smoke and debris that filled the air. Of course, for Sean, talking to a friend about their own 9/11 experience or watching a news report, movie, or TV show that talks about the event causes his PTSD symptoms to kick in.

Once you recognize more of your own triggers, it's possible to train yourself to prepare for these situations and choose your response ahead of time. Over time, this will help reduce your symptoms.

EXERCISE **YOUR TRIGGERS**

For each of the following symptom categories, list anything you've noticed that triggers those symptoms in a way that impacts your health and wellness. Keep in mind that one trigger can initiate multiple symptoms, so you may list the same trigger in more than one category. You may even want to ask someone you trust to help you pinpoint any triggers they've observed.

Anxiety

Anger

Panic Attacks/Physiological Responses

Depression

Flashbacks and Intrusive Thoughts

Nightmares

Being aware of your triggers can help you put a plan in place to head them off before your symptoms become unmanageable.

WHAT ARE YOUR AVOIDANCE BEHAVIORS?

Five months ago, Davon was running on the treadmill at his gym when he had a heart attack. Thankfully, a trainer acted quickly and administered CPR. Davon is healing well after having open-heart surgery, and his doctor cleared him to return to his workouts, suggesting that walking on the treadmill would help his recovery. However, he can't imagine returning to the gym or getting back on the treadmill.

Urges to avoid are a natural response to traumatic experiences. Avoiding danger is instinctual, especially when your experience was life-threatening. It can feel counter-intuitive to return to a situation that you associate with that life-or-death experience. You may experience strong physiological reactions when you attempt to approach a triggering situation and feel that the activity is "impossible."

Many avoidance behaviors negatively impact your health and wellness, such as using drugs, alcohol, or food to regulate your emotions; avoiding medical or therapy appointments; refusing to go to your house of worship because you feel guilt or shame; not wanting to work out; or avoiding regular health monitoring or treatments. You may use escape by cutting your workouts short, using a smoke break as a way to get out of a stressful situation, or arriving at an appointment for a health provider but leaving before your appointment begins. Let's take a look at some of the avoidance behaviors you use that could be impacting your health and well-being.

EXERCISE YOUR AVOIDANCE BEHAVIORS

Contemplate your health and wellness avoidance behaviors. In this worksheet, list your avoidance behaviors in the first column. In the second column, identify the situations in which you use those behaviors to cope.

AVOIDANCE BEHAVIOR	I USE THIS BEHAVIOR WHEN . . .

Sleep and Your Health

Sleep disturbances, especially insomnia and nightmares, are extremely common and among the most problematic symptoms of PTSD. Not only are they exhausting, but they're also very difficult to treat—often continuing even after your other trauma-related symptoms have responded to treatment.

According to the National Center for PTSD website, more than 90 percent of people with PTSD experience some form of sleep disturbance. Insomnia is the most common and can include difficulty falling asleep, frequent awakening, difficulty falling back to sleep, and waking up too early. Not only does insomnia make your nights miserable, it also leaves you fatigued and unable to function properly during the day. In addition, sleep deprivation can worsen other symptoms, including depression, anger, and difficulty with concentration.

Coupled with insomnia, the majority of trauma survivors also report nightmares. Some are so severe that not only do you wake up in a heightened state of fear, but you might call out, thrash about, fall out of bed, or injure yourself. This can create issues with bed partners who might be unable to sleep because of the disruptions or because they fear that you might hurt yourself or them. This can become so troublesome that you may feel like you have to sleep alone. It's even possible to become so distressed by nightmares that you're afraid to sleep at all.

There are steps you can take to address your sleep difficulties. Here are some to consider:

- Maintain a regular sleep schedule, including a regular time for going to bed at night and rising in the morning.

- Avoid sources of bright light (electronic screens or televisions) during the hours you've reserved for sleep.

- Limit caffeine and nicotine consumption; avoid these substances entirely during the afternoon and evening.

- Eat regularly scheduled healthy meals. Avoid heavy, spicy, or rich meals close to bedtime.

- Exercise vigorously early in the day (best before 2 p.m.) and avoid exercise near bedtime.

- Expose yourself to natural light in the morning to help set your natural circadian rhythm.

- Avoid relying on alcohol and other non-prescription substances for sleep. They may help you fall asleep, but they impair the quality and quantity of your sleep.

- Reserve your bed for sleep and sex only. Leave your bed for other activities, like reading or watching TV.

- Leave your bed if you aren't able to fall asleep within 10 to 15 minutes. Engage in quiet activity (reading, listening to music, prayer, or meditation) until you feel sleepy again. Then return to bed.

- Avoid daytime napping. If you must nap, limit your rest to 20 to 30 minutes. This will be enough to refresh you without interfering with your ability to fall asleep at your normal bedtime.

- Maintain a consistent pre-bedtime ritual consisting of activities like taking a warm bath or shower and quiet time.

- Keep your bedroom dark, quiet, and at a slightly cool but comfortable temperature.

- Eliminate distractions, such as pets or television in your bedroom.

- Turn your clock away from you. You don't want to become anxious about the amount of sleep you are or aren't getting.

- If you think you have sleep apnea (you snore loudly or intermittently stop breathing while sleeping), seek a medical evaluation because it may be disturbing the quality of your sleep.

If you consistently try the preceding suggestions for several weeks without success, see a doctor or mental health professional for a sleep evaluation. Other treatment options for sleep include:

- Cognitive-Behavioral Therapy for Insomnia (CBT-I)—This evidence-based treatment for insomnia uses cognitive-behavioral techniques to help you quiet your mind and relearn healthy sleep behaviors.

- Imagery Rehearsal Therapy (IRT) or Exposure, Relaxation, Rescripting Therapy (ERRT)—These evidence-based treatments can reduce the frequency and intensity of nightmares.

- Prescription medications will not cure sleep problems and can sometimes contribute to sleep disorders over time. However, some prescription medications offer relief from insomnia and/or nightmares.

HOW IS AVOIDANCE WORKING FOR YOU?

Think about the coping habits you identified in the previous exercise. You developed these strategies over time, and while they provide relief from your symptoms, they can negatively impact your health and wellness. For example, maybe you avoid thinking about your trauma by binge-watching endless seasons of one TV show after another. You may feel immediate relief from your symptoms but sitting on the couch and watching hours of TV every day will eventually damage your physical health due to inactivity. And, over time, this type of avoidance can lead to further challenges in your closest relationships and in other life domains. All of these challenges can impact your mental and spiritual health as well.

EXERCISE YOUR AVOIDANCE GAINS AND LOSSES

It's important to recognize the positives and negatives associated with the health and wellness avoidance strategies you've been relying on. That way, you can anticipate potential challenges as you begin to change your behavior. Respond to the following prompts in the spaces provided.

Describe a health or wellness situation that triggers an avoidance behavior and explain exactly how you react.

_____

_____

_____

_____

What are the payoffs for avoiding this situation?

_____

_____

What are the negatives of avoiding this situation?

WHAT ARE YOUR ALTERNATIVES?

To align your behavior with your values and goals, you need to recognize the positive and negative consequences of the behaviors you use to cope in stressful situations. You can choose to follow your values, even in uncomfortable situations. But don't worry if your behavior isn't where you want it to be or if you find yourself using avoidance the next time you're in a stressful situation. This process takes time. Break complicated tasks down into smaller chunks and go slowly.

Look at what successful coping strategies you already have in place to see if you can use them for other problem areas. For example, if you are able to stop intrusive memories at work by deliberately focusing on each detail of an assignment, try involving yourself in an absorbing task, such as preparing a healthy, multistep meal, when you're struggling with unwanted thoughts.

If you're reading the life sections out of order, go back to page 58 in section 3 for more detailed information on this topic before moving on to the following exercise.

Review the avoidance behaviors you identified in the exercise "Your Avoidance Behaviors" on page 135 that have negative consequences on your health and wellness. It's time to consider your alternatives. Respond to the following prompts in the spaces provided.

Think about the negative consequences or costs of your avoidance behaviors. How do they interfere with your long-term goals?

(For example: I use unhealthy habits to cope with stress. When I've had a bad day, I stop to get fast food on the way home and usually eat the whole bag of food while I'm driving. I drink a few beers and eat snacks while I sit on the sofa watching TV for the rest of the night. This interferes with my goals because I want to lose weight, but these behaviors are making it impossible.)

What could you try instead? List three to five options for alternative responses.

(For example: I could wait to eat a healthy meal when I get home. I could go for a run after work or take the dog for a long walk. I could refrain from drinking alcohol on weeknights and try to keep my snacking to a minimum.)

EXERCISE   BREAKING DOWN TARGET BEHAVIORS

Refer back to the challenge areas you identified in the exercise "Uncovering Target Behaviors" on page 130. Choose a behavior to target. Every time you practice your target behavior, you will be building a new habit.

In this exercise, you'll identify some smaller goals or steps you can take to increase your chance of success. Some of these steps may be uncomfortable and require multiple repetitions before you're ready to move on to the next step. Fill in all of your anticipated difficulty ratings now, before you even begin to practice them. It's okay if some of your numbers are very high—they will decrease as you practice.

If one of your steps involves doing the activity with someone you know, it's a good idea to explain what you're doing before you start. This will help them understand your behavior if you get uncomfortable and also make it easier for you to stay on track.

Here is an example to get you started:

Target Behavior: I don't abuse drugs or alcohol.

Specific Goal: Reduce the amount of alcohol I drink to cope with stressful situations.

STEPS I CAN TAKE RIGHT NOW TO REACH MY GOAL	ANTICIPATED DIFFICULTY 0 = easy, 5 = moderately uncomfortable, 10 = impossible
Create a daily alcohol log and commit to writing down every drink I consume and any stress I was experiencing or expecting before I took my first sip.	4
If I drink alcohol daily, I will reduce the number of drinks I have by one per day.	7
Establish an alcohol-free day each week and engage in a pleasurable activity that doesn't involve drinking during the same time period I would normally drink; increase the number of alcohol-free days over time.	7
If I routinely meet up with friends for drinks at the end of the day, suggest a different activity that doesn't involve alcohol.	6
If I normally consume multiple drinks in a row, I will slowly drink one glass of water or another nonalcoholic beverage after every alcoholic beverage.	6

Target Behavior:

....

Specific Goal:

....

STEPS I CAN TAKE RIGHT NOW TO REACH MY GOAL	ANTICIPATED DIFFICULTY 0 = easy, 5 = moderately uncomfortable, 10 = impossible

Now that you have an idea of what steps you can take toward your target behavior, identify any obstacles you might encounter and how you will overcome them so that you have a plan in place.

What obstacles might prevent you from practicing?

(For example: My friends might not want to go somewhere that doesn't involve drinking alcohol.)

....

How can you overcome these obstacles?

(For example: I can reach out to an acquaintance or family member to do something different with me if my regular group of friends doesn't want to change the plan.)

....

EXERCISE   ACTION PLAN FOR CHANGE

It's time to create a health and wellness action plan to help you strategize and make key decisions before a triggering situation arises. Some new behaviors will be immediately rewarding, such as eating a healthy breakfast each morning, but others will take time to showcase their benefits. To identify appropriate goals, consider your values (you will do this in the first step).

Values are important because they remind us of the direction we want to head in. After determining the direction you want to go, focus on identifying a moderately challenging goal and the type of reinforcement you'll need to stay motivated. Consider creating a reward system for practicing. This should be something you look forward to, like taking your dog for a walk or splurging on a nice cut of meat to barbecue for dinner. Figure out what will motivate you to keep moving forward, even when things become challenging.

STEP ONE

In section 2, you identified your top three values (see page 27). Reflect on these values and consider how they apply to your health and wellness. Ultimately, multiple values will come into play, but for now start with one you think is most important for this area and write it in the space provided.

Value:

STEP TWO

Think of a target behavior that relates to that value and identify your specific goal. Write them in the spaces provided. (Remember, if your target behavior doesn't have a set number of repetitions, try to practice a minimum of four times during the next week.)

Target Behavior:

Specific Goal:

STEP THREE

What problems or obstacles do you think you might encounter as you work toward your goal?

Problems/Obstacles: ....

STEP FOUR

What solutions or modifications can you try if problems or obstacles arise?

Solutions/Modifications: ....

STEP FIVE

What avoidance behaviors do you think you might want to participate in as you challenge yourself?

Potential Avoidance Behaviors: ....

STEP SIX

What can you try instead of the avoidance behaviors?

Alternatives to Avoidance Behaviors: ....

STEP SEVEN

What will reinforce your new behavior?

Behavior Reinforcement: ....

STEP EIGHT

Review the exercise "Breaking Down Target Behaviors" on page 141. In the space provided, write down the steps you can take to work up to your ultimate goal. These steps will help you identify new behaviors to target as you achieve mastery of your initial target behaviors.

Steps to Take:

1. ....

2. ....

3. ....

4. ....

5. ....

STEP NINE

When you reach your goal or complete your target behavior, what type of reward do you expect to receive? This may be a personal sense of accomplishment or satisfaction or some external reward, like a lower number on the scale.

Rewards for Success: ....

STEP TEN

In the following worksheet, record the results from your practice sessions. If necessary, review the exercise "Evaluating Your Progress" on page 40.

1. Record the date of each practice session.
2. Using the scale from the exercise "Degree of Difficulty" on page 38, fill in your anticipated difficulty levels and actual difficulty levels (0 = completely relaxed and at peace; 10 = most distressed, unable to think clearly, fight/flight/freeze response engaged).
3. Using the scale from the exercise "What Are You Doing Now?" on page 28, rate the levels of emotion you experienced while practicing the behavior (0 = complete lack of the emotion; 10 = a high level of the emotion).

4. After you've completed a few practice sessions, your difficulty levels and your depression/sadness and anxiety/irritability levels should decrease, while your pleasure/satisfaction levels should gradually increase. The idea is to continue working on the same target behavior until you notice substantial changes in your levels. It's okay if this takes longer than one week. Some very challenging behaviors may take several weeks to become more comfortable. Just keep working at it until you notice substantial changes. When one step becomes less challenging, you'll be ready to move on to the next step toward your goal.

DATE PRACTICED	ANTICIPATED DIFFICULTY (0–10)	ACTUAL DIFFICULTY (0–10)	DEPRESSION/ SADNESS (0–10)	ANXIETY/ IRRITABILITY (0–10)	PLEASURE/ SATISFACTION (0–10)	OTHER (0–10)

STEP ELEVEN

Once you've reached your goal, assess what went well and what didn't. Use that information to help decide which behavior to target next.

Next Target Behavior:

EXERCISE   YOUR HEALTH AND WELLNESS ACTION PLAN

Now let's take all the information you've gathered on your target behaviors, potential obstacles, and rewards and create an action plan for your first health and wellness goal.

Target Behavior:

Specific Goal:

Problems/Obstacles:

Solutions/Modifications:

Potential Avoidance Behaviors:

Alternatives to Avoidance Behaviors:

Behavior Reinforcement:

Steps to Take:

1. ....

2. ....

3. ....

4. ....

5. ....

Anticipated Rewards for Success: ....

DATE PRACTICED	ANTICIPATED DIFFICULTY (0–10)	ACTUAL DIFFICULTY (0–10)	DEPRESSION/ SADNESS (0–10)	ANXIETY/ IRRITABILITY (0–10)	PLEASURE/ SATISFACTION (0–10)	OTHER (0–10)

DATE PRACTICED	ANTICIPATED DIFFICULTY (0–10)	ACTUAL DIFFICULTY (0–10)	DEPRESSION/ SADNESS (0–10)	ANXIETY/ IRRITABILITY (0–10)	PLEASURE/ SATISFACTION (0–10)	OTHER (0–10)

Next Target Behavior:

<hr>

EXERCISE   **REVIEWING YOUR PROGRESS**

Now that you've set an initial goal for health and wellness and practiced your target behavior, let's assess your progress. Respond to the following prompts in the spaces provided:

How did you feel when you completed this goal?

Were there any unexpected challenges? If so, what were they?

Was anything easier than expected?

_____

_____

_____

How did you overcome the obstacles you encountered?

_____

_____

_____

Should you try to take on a less challenging task next time, or are you ready to increase the intensity?

_____

_____

_____

How difficult will it be to maintain your new behavior?

_____

_____

_____

How can you overcome obstacles that could interfere with engaging in this behavior in the future?

....

....

....

TAKEAWAYS

- Your physical, emotional, and spiritual health are all impacted by your PTSD symptoms.
- Depression, anxiety, insomnia, and other PTSD symptoms make functioning very difficult and contribute to challenges with your physical and mental health.
- Research has shown that trauma survivors have higher incidences of physical health challenges than others.
- Sleep disturbances are some of the most challenging symptoms of PTSD.
- Many avoidance behaviors can significantly interfere with your ability to keep yourself healthy and well.

STAYING THE COURSE

LONG-TERM OUTLOOK

As we near the end of this workbook, we want to take a moment to recognize the effort you've made toward building a healthier future for yourself. Congratulations on your work so far—no doubt much of it has been challenging and even uncomfortable. Trauma is a life-altering experience that fundamentally shifts the way you view yourself, others, and the world.

By completing the different sections of this workbook, you've gained a better understanding of the full impact trauma has had on all aspects of your life. By working hard and committing to your goals, you've probably started to notice that the intensity and frequency of some of your symptoms has already decreased. As you continue to try out new behaviors, get back to old activities you'd abandoned, or simply become more active and engaged, you'll keep making progress toward living the life you want to live.

Obviously, there's still more to do. PTSD is a long-term condition that will throw you an occasional curveball right when you're least expecting it. Stress or a significant life challenge can cause your symptoms to flare up temporarily, even after a long period of improvement. But you shouldn't worry; this doesn't mean you've failed—it simply means you're normal. When you're triggered in the future, remember that you've created a personal PTSD tool kit that has helped you get to this point and can help you overcome any return of symptoms you might face in the future.

In this final section, you'll assess your progress, identify goals for the future, and proactively problem-solve for any obstacles that may arise. You'll create a plan that will carry you forward, helping you stay on track, reaching one goal after another, and reducing your symptoms with each achievement.

Whether you've stuck to your plan without faltering along the way or had moments where you threw your hands in the air and gave up—you're here now. And you've made progress. We know that this is tough. We also know that it's worth the hard work and dedication. Congratulations on making it this far. We're in your corner and ready to help you take this process to the next level.

TARGETING YOUR BIGGEST CHALLENGES

After the anniversary weekend that got derailed by his symptoms, John's wife encouraged him to tackle his PTSD head-on. He researched his options and decided that behavioral activation sounded like the best fit for him. At first it was challenging, and he ran into several roadblocks that almost made him quit, but he persisted and underwent a major transformation.

He considers himself to be a work in progress and can't imagine giving up now. He's sleeping better, rarely has nightmares, and has learned how to manage the intrusive thoughts and panic symptoms that used to get him off track. He's making an effort to socialize outside of his home and recently took his sons to an amusement park for the first time. He couldn't believe how much fun they had; months before, he couldn't have imagined enjoying such a noisy, crowded place.

John has stopped overeating when stressed and walks the dog for an hour every night after dinner. He feels good with where he's at in life. Occasionally, something triggers him, but he uses the skills he's learned and the symptoms are generally short lived and not as strong as before.

Then one evening after dinner, he and his wife are watching the local news when a story comes on about a man arrested for molesting multiple children in the area. John's wife grabs for the remote, but before she can turn off the TV, the man's neighbors and relatives are being interviewed. Every one of them claims that the man they know would never do something like this.

Over the next few days, John can't sleep because every waking moment is filled with horrible memories of the night he was molested. John has no idea who these children are, but he can feel their pain and confusion so acutely that it causes his heart rate to spike, and several times he has chest pains and shortness of breath. He has terrible nightmares when he does sleep. His thoughts are jumbled, and he can't focus. In addition, John is angry. He's angry with his uncle and with the man whose mug shot he saw on TV. He's angry with the relatives who didn't believe him all those years ago. He's angry with himself and wonders if he could have done or said something differently that would have helped put his uncle behind bars. John has never felt anger like this before. It burns with a constant fury and nothing he does makes it go away. He avoids spending time with anyone because he worries about what he might say or do to anyone who happens to be around when he finally erupts.

By the end of the week, John is exhausted and desperate to relieve his symptoms. He decides to try using the behavioral activation tools he's learned in recent years. Even though he doesn't feel like it, he resumes his normal routines. He practices mindfulness and grounding, and, although it's very tough at first, it takes only a few days before his symptoms begin to decrease.

As you've started making changes in your life, you've probably noticed some are more easily done than others. We're all creatures of habit so changing our routines can be difficult. Knowing how your different behaviors fit into your personal values helps make the process a little smoother. You'll be more successful if you make a conscious effort to stick to your goals, evaluating your behavior on a daily basis so that you don't fall back into old habits like John did when he was triggered.

To make a lasting change, you'll need to maintain your new habits while continuing to set more challenging goals. You still have work ahead of you, and some of it is going to be hard—especially when you tackle your most firmly entrenched habits—but you only need to take one step at a time.

Once you've committed to a new behavior, such as going to the gym, reading to your kids before bed, or practicing mindfulness, you'll notice that the more consistently you put your new habit into practice, the more natural it will become. However, if you let up, it's easy to slip back into your old pattern of behaviors. Keep pushing yourself to move forward. If your goal is to run five miles, but you stop pushing yourself to run any farther than two, you're going to hit a plateau and fail to reach your goal. The same thing is true for all of your goals.

At this point, you've learned to identify the obstacles and triggers that trouble you the most. Maybe you've learned that you're less likely to attend your morning class if you stay up late, or you don't make it to the gym if your gym clothes are dirty. Take note of any roadblocks you've encountered. Planning for them will help you succeed as you create new habits.

Even so, not all obstacles and triggers can be anticipated. Some of the most powerful challenges you will face are the ones you don't see coming. They will catch you off guard and make it difficult to stay on course. The good news is that by learning the skills in this book, you'll gain confidence in your ability to survive the unexpected and you'll have the tools in place to deal with any new challenges that surface.

Life is unpredictable and you will experience stress in the future. Even when you think you've resolved some of your trauma-related symptoms, relationship difficulties, failures at work or school, or the illness of a family member can cause them to flare up. It's even possible that you might have another traumatic experience. Unfortunately, any of these things or something you've never even considered may make you feel like you've gone back to the beginning. Just remember that a return or worsening of symptoms is normal in these circumstances. If this happens to you, take a deep breath, review what you've learned, and dig into your toolbox. You can do this.

EXERCISE   PLANNING FOR ROADBLOCKS

Think about everything you've learned about triggers. You've worked on how to deal with them when they crop up. You've read about things that trigger other trauma survivors and have certainly experienced a wide range of triggering events as you've been working your way through this book. Now, respond to the following prompt:

What situations are likely to trigger you in the future?

1.

2.

3.

4.

5.

6.

7.

8.

9.

10.

FINDING WHAT WORKS FOR YOU

Now that you have a list of situations that might trigger you in the future, and you've reviewed all of the skills in this workbook, you have the tools you need to continue your return to the valued activities you gave up after your traumatic experience, to move forward toward achieving your goals, and to deal with the curveballs life is bound to throw at you.

You don't need to master all of the skills offered in this book to be successful. Think about everything you've tried and keep what works best. These tools may be sufficient as you continue the process, or you may be ready to try learning some additional skills. Just as PTSD is a little bit different for each individual, so is effective coping.

Here are some strategies you may want to have in your personal toolbox:

- Keeping a consistent schedule
- Using grounding to cope with stressful situations
- Making commitments for action to yourself and others
- Practicing mindfulness or meditation
- Accessing social support
- Practicing tasks that bring a sense of mastery
- Remembering that your brain may respond to safe situations as if they're dangerous
- Telling yourself that you're "okay" when you experience a "false alarm"
- Taking care of your personal health
- Monitoring progress toward long- and short-term goals
- Appreciating the progress you've made and the good things in your life
- Exposing yourself to situations you've avoided so you can learn that they are safe

YOUR TOOLBOX OF SKILLS

Now think about what works for you and, in the space provided, make a list of your most successful tools below. In the future, when you're struggling with symptoms or having trouble reaching a goal, look at your list and try as many of these tools as you need to in order to succeed.

1. ....

2. ....

3. ....

4. ....

5. ....

RELAPSE PREVENTION

There will probably come a point in your journey where you relapse, falling back into old habits and ways of coping. Sometimes a relapse occurs gradually when you believe that your changes are well established and you relax your efforts a little. But it can also happen suddenly when you encounter environmental stress or triggering situations, just like it did for John in the scenario earlier in this chapter.

Some things that can trigger a relapse include:

- Relationship difficulties
- Work/school problems
- Financial concerns
- Housing difficulties
- Health problems
- Worries about the well-being of a loved one
- A triggering event
- Experiencing another trauma

Relapse is very common, so you should be prepared for it. Don't beat yourself up if it happens; it's a very normal part of the recovery process. Just get back to your plan and work to regain control of your symptoms again. That said, there are steps you can take to help prevent relapse, such as:

- Build strong external support for your new habits.
- Address environmental stressors, such as relationship issues, financial concerns, work/school issues, etc.
- Find healthy, rewarding, daily activities to do alone or with others.
- Attend to your physical and mental health by keeping follow-up appointments, taking medication as prescribed, and following medical advice.
- Maintain healthy habits, like eating balanced meals, following a sleep schedule, and exercising.
- Participate in activities that are physically and mentally engaging and bring a sense of mastery.

When you realize your symptoms or old coping behaviors are returning, pick up this book and review your plan. You've assembled a well-stocked toolbox that will help you refocus on what you need to do and how to do it. If the big picture is over-whelming or you feel discouraged, just do the *next* right thing. Use your values as a compass check. Stop and see where you are. If you've veered off course, simply correct your course and take one step at a time toward your goal.

EXERCISE   GOAL SETTING

Earlier in this workbook, you practiced setting initial goals and plotting out the small steps needed to reach them. Continuing this process should occupy you for the foreseeable future; however, we also want you to think about the bigger picture.

What are your biggest goals for the future? Right now, it's okay if you don't know all the steps it will take for you to get there. This is about having something big to reach for as you work through your smaller goals.

My biggest goals for the future are:

1.

2.

3.

4.

5.

Safety Plan

For some people who experience trauma, extremely intense and uncomfortable thoughts and feelings can make it difficult for them to believe that things will get better, and they may think it would be easier to give up. While those types of moments will pass and you will feel hope again, you may feel overwhelmed and alone when they are happening. That's why it's a good idea to have a plan in place as a type of safety insurance policy for these moments.

Complete this safety plan and keep it in an easily accessible place (the refrigerator, your desk drawer, or your glove box). When you experience overwhelming emotions, it is difficult to think clearly and remember that you have tools to help you make it through a crisis. By having a safety plan in place, you can move through the items on your plan when you need them.

If you cannot maintain your commitment to safety or are considering self-harm, use the emergency contacts and national hotline numbers listed in the Resources section on page 165. Trained professionals are available to help you 24 hours a day. If you need to speak to someone right now, call **National Suicide Prevention Lifeline: 1-800-273-8255 (TALK).**

Situations that can trigger intense thoughts, feelings, or urges for self-harm (e.g., anniversary dates, nightmares, and trauma reminders):

_____

_____

_____

_____

Things I can do to help myself feel better during a crisis (e.g., spending time with a pet, being outdoors, exercise, and prayer):

_____

_____

_____

_____

Activities with others that can help during a crisis (e.g., call a friend, spend time with family, and visit a safe public place):

_____

_____

_____

_____

Supportive people I can contact:

Name
_____

Phone Number
_____

Name
_____

Phone Number
_____

Name
_____

Phone Number
_____

Name
_____

Phone Number
_____

Professional members of my support team (e.g.,
physician, therapist, case manager, clergyperson):

Name
_____

Phone Number
_____

Name
_____

Phone Number
_____

Name
_____

Phone Number
_____

Name
_____

Phone Number
_____

Things I can do to create a safe environment
(e.g., avoid drugs and alcohol, spend time with
others, avoid risky/compulsive behaviors, and give
weapons to support people for safekeeping):

_____

_____

_____

_____

My biggest reason for living:

_____

_____

_____

_____

National Suicide Prevention Lifeline: 1-800-273-8255 (TALK)

FINDING SUPPORT

While it's up to you to do the hard work, a critical part of your success depends on the strength of support you have from the people around you. Whether you already have some of these supportive relationships or are working to develop them in the future, relying on them will help get you through the rough spots. It doesn't matter if support comes from your partner, friends, family members, clergy, coworkers, classmates, or neighbors. Just work on building a strong, supportive network of people you can count on and who can count on you in return.

It can be comforting to connect with other trauma survivors or people with similar recovery goals. The more you tell others about your experience, goals, and type of support you want, the more you'll find secure and stable sources of support.

If you've isolated yourself or used avoidance extensively, your current network may be limited. This may also be true if you've been depressed or angry and have pushed others away. Regardless, part of getting active for you will include increasing your personal contacts. It's okay to start small. Say hello to a neighbor or coworker or reach out to someone in an online forum. In-person or online support groups can also provide support when you need it most.

Take notice of the people currently in your life who already offer steady support. PTSD can be difficult to understand, even when you're the one suffering from it. Not everyone will be a good source of support. Others around you will have their own reactions to your traumatic experience or have their own personal struggles to deal with that make it difficult for them to offer the kind of help you need. Support from a loved one may come in the form of a comforting hand during Fourth of July fireworks, time spent together after a difficult day, a friend accompanying you to the doctor, or a knowing look when you seem at the end of a short fuse.

Appreciate the people who are supportive and find compassion for them when they fall short or have their own difficulties. Supporting someone with PTSD is challenging, and your loved ones are probably suffering in response to your pain and suffering. Keep in mind that there will be times that the support you need may not come in the package you expect. Support may be your 12-Step sponsor insisting you attend a meeting, or your spouse telling you to get out of bed and drive your child to school. Think about why they're asking you to do something uncomfortable and recognize that it may be the exact encouragement you need.

Asking for, and sometimes even accepting, support requires vulnerability. If someone were physically injured, you'd need to know where it hurt before you could provide first aid. PTSD is tough because there's no physical mark. You may look okay on the outside even though you're struggling. This is very confusing for everyone around you. It doesn't mean that others can't or won't rise to the occasion and offer what you need, but ultimately, it's not their job to take charge of your recovery—it's yours. Even if your trauma occurred through no fault of your own or in the service of others, your symptoms and your recovery are your responsibility.

A FEW FINAL WORDS

Trauma recovery is like a giant puzzle—when you first dump the box on the table, you can't see any matching pieces; they're all jumbled together in one big messy pile. After a moment, you start to see the edge pieces sticking up out of the chaos. You pick up one and then another. You begin connecting them together until you've created the basic frame that will guide you through the rest of the process. Then you look for colors that match, putting them into neat little piles until you figure out where they need to go. It takes time, but with patience and dedication, you put together one piece after another until you start to see the bigger picture. Suddenly, the oddly shaped middle pieces make sense and seem to fall into place all at once.

Just like with the puzzle, stand back for a moment and recognize what you've already accomplished. You have made amazing progress, even if you're not done yet. And, just like with the puzzle, if you want your hard work to last, you'll need to protect it and look out for anything that could take it apart. After all of your effort to put the puzzle together, you don't want the cat to jump on the table and knock it to the floor.

Don't give up and don't get discouraged if you encounter bumps along the way. Remember to focus on the reasons you decided to begin this process, take one slow step at a time, and keep your tools sharp and ready to go so that you can use them when needed.

You *can* do this. In fact, you already are.

RESOURCES

We hope that your journey toward recovery continues after you've completed this workbook. The organizations listed below offer a wealth of information and valuable resources for trauma survivors and their loved ones.

For Immediate Assistance

NATIONAL SUICIDE PREVENTION LIFELINE

If you are considering self-harm, this is the place to get help 24/7. It's free and confidential for anyone in crisis, and they will help you find resources in your area.

1-800-273-8255 (Press 1 for veterans)
Or text SIGNS to 741741 for the Crisis Text Line
www.suicidepreventionlifeline.org

NATIONAL DOMESTIC VIOLENCE HOTLINE

If you are experiencing domestic violence, you can find confidential help here 24/7. They will help you find resources or information, or question unhealthy aspects of your relationship.

1-800-799-7233
www.thehotline.org

NATIONAL SEXUAL ASSAULT HOTLINE

The hotline and website chat offer assistance to sexual assault survivors or concerned loved ones 24/7. They partner with more than 1,000 local sexual assault service providers around the country, operate the DoD Safe Helpline for the Department of Defense, help survivors, educate the public about sexual violence, and more.

1-800-656-HOPE (4673)
www.rainn.org

Information and Resources for Trauma Survivors

NATIONAL CENTER FOR PTSD

This organization is dedicated to trauma and PTSD research and education. Their website is an excellent source of information, including the latest research findings, for trauma survivors and their loved ones, veteran or non-veteran.

www.ptsd.va.gov

MAKE THE CONNECTION

This interactive website is specifically for veterans recovering from PTSD.

www.maketheconnection.net

1IN6

An online resource for men who have experienced sexual abuse or assault. It provides confidential chats with an advocate 24/7, online support groups, and information.

www.1in6.org

FIRST RESPONDER SUPPORT NETWORK

An organization dedicated to providing educational support for first responders and their families following a trauma.

1-415-721-9789
www.frsn.org

ABOUT FACE

This website is an excellent resource for anyone who wants to learn more about PTSD and various treatments. There are short, unscripted videos of veterans discussing their PTSD, family members explaining how their loved one's PTSD has impacted them, and providers who explain more about PTSD.

www.ptsd.va.gov/apps/AboutFace

GIVE AN HOUR

A network of mental health professionals who offer free services to military service members, veterans, and anyone impacted by natural or man-made disasters.

www.giveanhour.org/get-help

Online Resources for Self-Help

PTSD COACH

A mobile app designed to help learn about and manage symptoms of PTSD. It includes tools for screening and tracking symptoms, information on treatment options, tools for managing symptoms, and links to helpful resources.

www.ptsd.va.gov/public/materials/apps/ptsdcoach.asp

VET CHANGE

A free, confidential self-guided app designed to assist veterans in cutting back or discontinuing alcohol use and managing PTSD symptoms without using alcohol.

www.vetchange.org

Learn More About Treatment Options

US DEPARTMENT OF VETERANS AFFAIRS: NATIONAL CENTER FOR PTSD

To learn more about trauma-focused treatment, you can watch some short videos about treatment approaches for PTSD at www.ptsd.va.gov/public/materials/videos/index.asp.

www.ptsd.va.gov

REFERENCES

Dijk, Sheri Van. *DBT Made Simple: A Step-by-Step Guide to Dialectical Behavior Therapy*. Oakland, CA: New Harbinger Publications, 2013.

Hayes, Steven C. *Get Out of Your Mind and Into Your Life: The New Acceptance and Commitment Therapy*. Oakland, CA: New Harbinger Publications, 2005.

Imel, Zach E., Kevin Laska, Matthew Jakupcak, and Tracy L. Simpson. "Meta-Analysis of Dropout in Treatments for Posttraumatic Stress Disorder." *Journal of Consulting and Clinical Psychology* 81, no. 3 (June 2013): 394–404. doi:10.1037/a0031474.

Jakupcak, Matthew, Amy Wagner, Autumn Paulson, Alethea Varra, and Miles McFall. "Behavioral Activation as a Primary Care-Based Treatment for PTSD and Depression Among Returning Veterans." *Journal of Traumatic Stress* 23, no. 4 (August 2010): 491–95. doi:10.1002/jts.20543.

Kanter, Jonathan, Andrew M. Busch, and Laura C. Rusch. *Behavioral Activation: Distinctive Features*. New York: Routledge, 2009.

Kehle-Forbes, Shannon M., Laura A. Meis, Michele R. Spoont, and Melissa A. Polusny. "Treatment Initiation and Dropout from Prolonged Exposure and Cognitive Processing Therapy in a VA Outpatient Clinic." *Psychological Trauma: Theory, Research, Practice, and Policy* 8, no. 1 (June 2015): 107–14. doi:10.1037/tra0000065.

McFarlane, Alexander C. "The Long-Term Costs of Traumatic Stress: Intertwined Physical and Psychological Consequences." *World Psychiatry* 9, no. 1 (February 2010): 3–10. www.ncbi.nlm.nih.gov/pmc/articles/PMC2816923/.

Mulick, Patrick S., and Amy E. Naugle. "Behavioral Activation for Comorbid PTSD and Major Depression: A Case Study." *Cognitive and Behavioral Practice* 11, no. 4 (Autumn 2004): 378–387. www.sciencedirect.com/science/article/pii /S1077722904800543.

Najavits, Lisa M. "The Problem of Dropout from 'Gold Standard' PTSD Therapies." *F1000Prime Reports* 7 (April 2015): 43. doi:10.12703/p7-43.

Najavits, Lisa M. *Seeking Safety: A Treatment Manual for PTSD and Substance Abuse.* New York: Guilford Press, 2003.

PTSD: National Center for PTSD. "PTSD: National Center for PTSD." US Department of Veteran's Affairs. Accessed June 11, 2018. www.ptsd.va.gov/.

Society of Clinical Psychology. "Treatment: Behavioral Activation for Depression." Society of Clinical Psychology. Accessed June 11, 2018. www.div12.org/treatment /behavioral-activation-for-depression/.

Tolin, D. F., and Breslau, N. "Sex Differences in Risk of PTSD." *PTSD Research Quarterly* 18, no. 2 (2007): 1–8.

Turner, Aaron P., and Matthew Jakupcak. "Behavioral Activation for Treatment of PTSD and Depression in an Iraqi Combat Veteran with Multiple Physical Injuries." *Behavioural and Cognitive Psychotherapy* 38, no. 03 (May 2010): 355–61. doi:10.1017/s1352465810000081.

INDEX

ABOUT THE AUTHORS

Lisa Burgert Campbell, PhD, is a psychologist for the Department of Veterans Affairs. She currently serves as the Program Coordinator for the San Diego VA South County PTSD Program and is affiliated with the psychology training program at the University of California, San Diego. During the past 15 years, she's counseled all types of trauma survivors, both for the VA and in her private practice. In her spare time, she's happiest when hanging out with her husband and two sons.

Karie A. Kermath is a trauma survivor who successfully completed Prolonged Exposure for PTSD. After her life went rogue, she discovered the healing power of sharing her experiences with the world and helping others stare down their own symptoms of PTSD. When she's not blogging at at *The Vermilion Road*, she's out and about with her son, their two corgis, Barnaby and Watson, and Jasper, the cat-in-the-backpack.

CPSIA information can be obtained
at www.ICGtesting.com
Printed in the USA
BVHW02s1027060918
526494BV00002B/1/P